A SUDDEN

A SUDDEN MUSIC

Roger White

GEORGE RONALD
OXFORD

First published by
GEORGE RONALD, Publisher
46 High Street, Kidlington, Oxford OX5 2DN

ISBN 0-85398-162-0 (Hardcover)
ISBN 0-85398-163-9 (Softcover)

Set by Sunrise Setting in Bembo 12 on 13 point
Printed in England

NOTE

All characters in this work are historical save Althea Edison Benedict, Emily Prior, Maggie O'Connor, Michael Athlone and their families; Nels Erikson; Amy Summerville; Prof and Mme Clémenceau; Peter Alderton; the Stoughtons; Bertha Monroe; the poet, John Allister; and the musician, LeTellier.

The Bahá'ís mentioned in the text are among those whose names dot the pages of early issues of *Star of the West*. In many instances their lives and services are described in the 'In Memoriam' section of volumes of *The Bahá'í World*.

All the words directly attributed to 'Abdu'l-Bahá are from the following published sources: *Star of the West*, *'Abdu'l-Bahá in London*, *Paris Talks* and *The Diary of Juliet Thompson*.

To the memory of

May Ellis Maxwell

' 'Abdu'l‑Bahá's beloved handmaid . . .
distinguished disciple'

to whom is owed

'a debt of gratitude which future generations
will not fail to adequately recognize'

Shoghi Effendi

(Cablegram 3 March 1940
Message 15 April 1940)

All that the [early believers in Paris] knew of the Bahá'í Cause was what someone had told someone else, and thus the word was passed on . . . we had very little real information about the Teachings. We depended mostly upon our faith and on our feelings rather than on actual information. It was a time, however, of great spiritual romance and adventure. The great religious fire of the Cause was uppermost in our minds. We all sang, as it were, a lyric Spiritual Song, and like all youth the adventure and the new outlook created a tremendous enthusiasm in our hearts . . . having so little [written literature] we were obliged to dwell largely on the emotional plane. Dreams and visions frequently made up to us our lack of actual knowledge.

Paris, 1901
(Unpublished diary of
C.M.R., pp. 46–9)

Foreword

273 rue Royal
Montreal, Quebec
21 April 1983

George Ronald, Publisher
46 High Street
Kidlington, Oxford

Gentlemen,

Three years ago there came into my possession the following postscript to a letter written by Althea Edison Benedict (then of Paris) to my great aunt, the late Emily Alderton (née Newton-Prior) of New York. It is dated 9 March 1912:

'A postscript in haste, dear. I forgot to say that Michael's firm is publishing a trilingual edition of the libretto of LeTellier's new comic operetta "La Question de l'Or". Michael has been commissioned to provide the English translation and Nels the German. I've been asked by Michael to assist with a little song placed in the mouth of the

1

heroine, Nicole – "that infuriating and elusive woman" as Michael describes her. This is my attempt at transcribing Nicole's reply to Count Marchand who has promised, if she will give him her hand, that she may choose to be his slave or his sovereign. In the last act, of course, she runs off with a penniless law student who by one of those twists of plot acceptable in such musical confections is revealed as the Count's younger brother. Nicole sings:

I would not wish to be your slave
Who'd tremble at your darkening mien
And dance in veils to coax your smile
And grow to love the binding chain.

Nor would I wish to be your queen
For I have known some I've supposed
Found early graves, despite their power,
By some ambitious wench deposed.

If you would have me as I am
I'd pin a plume upon my hat
And give you all I have of love.
Just as I am – but how is that?

'I rather admire the high-spirited Nicole and don't find her the least infuriating. If she could answer her own question she would be free to choose.

'I must hurry this off, dear, and take the translation round to Michael, one of my final obligations before I leave Paris. It is wonderful to realize that I may put my pen away and for the last time close my writing case. What will follow next will be the cablegram announcing my arrival. I think tonight of all the letters I have written to you and my other dear ones during the past several months and smile at the recognition that I shall soon meet you face to face.

'How would you have me sign my last letter from Paris save, as always, "Love, Althea."'

Intrigued to discover more about the recipient of the letter, my great aunt Emily whom I scarcely knew, I began a search which brought to me from various sources a number of the letters of Althea Edison Benedict which cast some light on her relationship with my great aunt and the bond between them which was at its heart. Regrettably, Emily Alderton's letters have not survived.

Despite the gaps in the correspondence of Althea Edison Benedict with her family and Emily Alderton these documents may be of interest in the degree that they reflect the development in Paris of the first Bahá'í center in Europe founded, as you surely know, by May Ellis Maxwell in 1901. If you would care to examine the letters with a view to publishing them, kindly let me know. Their publication would, I feel, be a modest tribute to those early Bahá'ís who courageously threw aside the conventions of their days and who, though they had little actual knowledge or literature, were recreated by the call of Bahá'u'lláh and laboured with extraordinary devotion to establish His Faith.

It may interest you to know that I was unaware previously of my great aunt's affiliation with the Bahá'í Faith and that in searching out and editing these letters I investigated and have now embraced it. My wife and I are at present making plans to settle as Bahá'í pioneers in France where I hope to complete my medical studies.

I shall look forward to hearing from you.

Yours sincerely,
Anthony Newton-Prior III

P.S. I should explain that it was upon my learning that the founder of George Ronald, Mr David Hofman, accepted the Bahá'í Faith through May Maxwell in Montreal in the early 1930s that I felt emboldened to offer this correspondence to your firm.

Excerpts from the letters of
Althea Edison Benedict

Pension Duval
93 rue Raynouard
Paris

17 January 1909

My dear Mamma,

I missed you! I could fill the page with those
words and not convey how orphaned I felt during
Christmas week! It was so very good to receive
your three letters within the space of a few days
and to learn that you and papa spent such a happy
holiday season, marred only by your slight
indisposition. I trust that you are now fully
recovered and have greeted the New Year with
your customary cheerful spirits and zest. I can
well imagine how busy you must have been
preparing for guests and I do hope you did not
overtax your strength. It was touching to read
that my absence was 'felt by all, especially on the
Birthday of our Lord'. Indeed, it was a strange
experience for me to be so far away from you and
dear papa at Christmas! It pleased me that Paul

and Ada and the children were able to spend three days with you, and thinking of you kneeling at the crèche and seated about the family dining table, which I know was laden with all the usual delicacies of the season, brought me great comfort. The tree must have been beautiful! You described it so clearly that I could almost visualize it dressed in its Mandarin oranges and gold velvet bows. There could not have been its like in all Boston!

But you must not think that I was given over to loneliness or self-pity, for I was caught up in a pleasant whirl of activity. With classes at the Conservatory suspended for the holiday period, I was able to spend a luxurious amount of time with my friends. Prof and Mme Clémenceau invited a small group of us to dine on Christmas Eve, and I spent the following day with the Stoughtons who had gathered up some homesick American friends, including Mr and Mrs Anthony Newton-Prior and their niece, Emily, of Boston. (Emily has shed the hyphen and is known simply as Emily Prior; I liked her on sight!) It turned out that although 'Mr and Mrs N-P' have lived in London for several years we have a mutual friend in Bertha Monroe. It was delightful to have this touch of 'home' and I must soon write to Bertha and tell her how affectionately she is remembered by these nice people. I say 'nice'; I was attracted instantly to Emily and found Mrs N-P quite charming and attractive, but her husband seemed rather opinionated and had little good to say of London. He styles himself an industrial economics consultant – whatever that may be! – and his long monologues about 'marginal utility' and 'the market', unintelligible to me, would have put me to sleep had not the Stoughtons, ably abetted by the courageous and outspoken Emily, skilfully diverted the conversation to subjects of more general interest. We were rescued at the point when Mr N-P was about to embark upon a discussion of the shortcomings of President Roosevelt's Commission on Import Controls, a subject rather too esoteric for the drawing room.

I was happy to learn that Emily will be remaining in Paris to attend *l'Académie des Beaux-Arts* – I'm sure we shall become fast friends. She is lovely, with hair of pale honey and startlingly blue eyes. I feel stolid beside her; she is very slight and moves with angular grace like a frisky kitten.

And, mamma, I seem to have made a *conquest* – without a conscious intention of doing so, I assure you! Among the guests was a young poet from New York, Nels Erikson, who belongs to a newly-formed group of writers calling themselves 'neo-Hellenists'. They are experimenting with new forms of writing, including *vers libre*, and are much influenced by Greek, Hebrew and Japanese poetic styles. Mr Erikson who is quite attractive and even *looks* like my idea of a poet is something of a crusader, I suspect. He spoke forcefully of the need for modern poets to bring to an end the domination of the novel as the principal literary form, to free themselves from the conventions of rhyme and meter, to avoid superfluous adjectives and pictorial description. He calls for the new poetry to be written in the concise and direct language of everyday speech, filled with tension, authentic feeling and sharp images, rather than – as he expressed it – to retain 'limp symbolism' and 'spurious emotion'.

You will note how well I paid attention to his remarks, but this was in part because Emily, I saw at once, pretended not to understand his point and, with a perfectly straight face and to considerable comic effect, kept asking him in an excessively earnest tone to interpret various poems of Wordsworth, Keats and Longfellow. She would then quote passages, deliberately garbling them. Gradually, of course, everyone with the possible exception of Emily's uncle, who seems mystified by anything that does not place him in the center of conversation, understood that she was joking, and one by one their eyes lit up as they sat back to enjoy the fun.

In order not to burst out laughing in the boy's face, thus proving myself not only rude but unappreciative of Emily's teasing which seemed harmless enough, I had to concentrate very closely upon Mr Erikson's words and in doing so composed my face in an attitude of the utmost sympathy and exaggerated attention. No doubt this caused him to feel that I was the only one present who understood him. Finally, after a particularly loud sigh of exasperation at one of Emily's silly remarks, the poet caught on and joined us in expressing amusement – it was such a relief to laugh aloud at last. But the damage was done. Mr Erikson remained convinced that my fixed staring at him had some deep meaning. He was most attentive to me for the remainder of the evening and a few days later presented me with one of his poems for which he said I was the inspiration. Should I avert my eyes and blush? I set it out for you, but I do not imagine that you will find the poem to your taste. Perhaps, however, it illustrates the point he was making.

> I reach out my longing hand
> and brush your gentle face,
> a pale white violet
> against my mossy palm.
> Your eyes gaze out
> to some far point
> beyond my misted glance.
> What star, my fair one,
> leads you home?
> What star do you await, Althea?

I am afraid that papa who so loves the classics will be outraged. As for me, I find the form rather appealing, although I shall forever remain suspicious of the *real* cause of the inspiration of poets.

In the brief time I have been in Paris my French appears to have improved – or perhaps I have simply grown oblivious to my distortions of pronunciation. Nevertheless, I use it with increasing confidence and Prof Clémenceau winces only occasionally. He is, however, considerably less charitable about my German which he describes as lamentably defective. When I attempt *lieder* he advises me (his great white mustache twitching irresistibly, causing him to look for all the world like a disapproving walrus) that my accent detracts from what he calls 'the fluid, molten quality' of

9

my voice. Thus I am encouraged and chastised in equal measure. The French art song, he feels, will be my true métier and he urges me to dedicate myself to its study.

Emily and I have agreed to meet from time to time as our studies permit. I am eager to see her paintings. She is a delightful companion, with a quick and inquisitive mind, and I thoroughly enjoy being with her. She has invited me to attend a meeting of the Theosophical Society in whose teachings she has recently developed an interest; and Nels Erikson has invited us both to a poetry reading sponsored by his circle of friends (Emily has promised to behave herself!). So my life is busy and full, and you and papa must not worry about me nor feel that I am lonely.

I feel very fortunate to have such loving and generous parents. It is a wonderful thing to be young and to be living in Paris where there is so much to do and see – the opera, ballet, the galleries – and to be surrounded by interesting friends. Sometimes I could almost hug myself with excitement, as though I were on the threshold of a great adventure.

Remember that you are in my thoughts and prayers. I send you both my deepest love. I miss my piano, my room, my books, the garden. But most of all I miss you.

P.S. Please reassure our Maggie that she is correct in thinking French cooking is, as she says, 'quite tasty' – but it isn't a patch on hers. I certainly have every intention of following her advice in not letting 'them foreigners be the ruination of my palate with all their garlic.' I have some scenic views for her and will send them along soon.

As ever,

Althea

———————

Paris
12 February 1909

Dear Mamma,

I was absolutely thrilled with the light wool shawl which you sent – such a lovely shade of lilac! – and I know I shall wear it often when the weather warms up a little. My grey serge cape is my constant uniform and a stalwart ally against the spiteful damp of Paris.

I am sorry that you were disturbed by my letter describing the meetings of the Theosophical Society that Emily and I attended. If I sounded enthusiastic it is because the discussion of their teachings stimulated and interested me, but I have not considered identifying myself with them. There is surely good in all things if we will only investigate and open our minds to benign influence. With the solid foundation of Christian principles and virtues you have provided me, how can I go astray? I enjoy the association with the people at these meetings; they have a thirst for spiritual knowledge and appear to live exemplary lives. There is, I am sure you will agree, much of truth and wisdom in the philosophies of the East.

But rest assured that I weigh all things carefully.

Emily and I discuss such questions for hours – our desire for knowledge and our love of beauty are a great bond between us. We share the conviction that there has been released into the world a new impulse, a creative force, that is being reflected in every area of human thought and endeavor including, of course, the arts; perhaps even especially the arts. Nels Erikson and his group are part of it, I suppose, and whatever one thinks of the result of their experimentation, one must admire their need and desire to experiment and encourage their efforts to find a new means of expressing truth as they see and experience it. Whatever force has been unleashed must be, I feel, benevolent and constructive. Perhaps it will lead to a greater understanding among the people of the world. I do not say this to shock or startle you, but because I feel so strongly that something wonderful is happening in the universe. I sense it so keenly here in Paris; sometimes my heart pounds with expectancy, as though at any moment I might turn a corner and it – something undefined and amazing – would be there awaiting me on an ordinary street under the everyday sky. This is a marvelous city, the very air is charged with excitement. I must hush, or you will think me overwrought.

Emily is crushed. She turned in a series of lovely pastel landscapes in which she had achieved splendid, innovative effects of light, and her instructor dismissed them with the caustic comment that she 'must not overreach her nice *little* talent!' She revenged herself by secretly executing a most devastating caricature of him in which he is shown on a step ladder counting the leaves on a tree in preparation for sketching it. She has given me one of her landscapes and I cherish it.

Nels and his friends are very excited about a poem written by a young American, Ezra Pound, which he feels points a new direction in contemporary writing. It bears the ominous title 'Revolt Against the Crepuscular Spirit in Modern Poetry.' I enclose a copy for you, though I fear you may find it offensive. Nels believes that one of the roles of the poet is to give spiritual direction to society and to define its goals, to intuit and prophesy its future. He is very tender and sensitive and I quite like him, although he lacks a ready sense of humor as do some highly intelligent people who see life as a Very Serious Business. He has written another poem for me – do you like it?

> The last listening red leaf
> falls from the lonely tree
> in a sad and silent saraband.
> I bend to it
> as I might lean to stroke your russet hair
> but a jealous breeze carries it
> beyond my touch,
> beyond my hunger.

He tells me it has been accepted for publication by his group's magazine, *Modernités* – I shall be notorious! But I trust not to a degree or for a cause that would embarrass you and papa. Emily reminds me, with appropriate scorn, that posterity is not only fickle but singularly indifferent to the juvenilia of minor poetizers. She is distrustful of Nels and rather guarded with him, but when I press her to tell me why she cannot explain. I grow fonder of her every day; she is all I could have hoped to find in a sister.

I had a disconcerting dream two nights ago – Maggie, I know, will attribute it to my eating cheese before retiring, but I suspect will also consult her dream book – in which I returned to Boston to visit you and found our house enveloped in a thick fog. Although I could hear your voices within, I could not gain entrance because the doors and windows had been sealed over. I kept circling the house in growing panic, calling your names aloud, but could not make myself heard. I have never felt so cold and frightened and alone. Then I heard Maggie call out as though in greeting in the moment that the dream dissolved, and I awakened to discover that the cold was real enough. I had thrown off the bed coverlet in my sleep and a damp breeze was blowing through the open window of my room.

———

Paris
2 March 1909

My dear Maggie,

It was a pleasure to have your letter for I think of you often. You would be truly surprised to know how frequently your dear, smiling face comes into my mind, or an echo of your warm voice filled with sensible advice. How good of mamma to share my news with you so that you can 'keep an eye' on me, as you say, even from this distance.

Mamma has written, too, about the long and severe winter, and I'm so sorry there has been so much sickness in your family. I trust all are feeling better now. The death of your young nephew, Timmy, must have been a cruel shock; he was such a merry little boy. Influenza is such a ruthless ally of Death and has brought so many little ones to the grave prematurely. I have remembered Timmy in my prayers, and I pray each day for you.

I am pleased that the other children enjoyed the scenic cards and I'll send you some others which may help them in their studies. Paris must seem very far away and not quite real to them. When I was young I imagined all the far-sounding cities of Europe and Asia to be made of spun sugar.

It was most thoughtful of you to make for me the little chamois-leather bag with draw-strings to carry my emergency money in when I go into the streets. I shall heed your warning and wear it *exactly* where you suggested! It is a sweet gift and I value it all the more knowing that you stitched it with such affection.

Will you send me your recipe for tea cake? I have a mind to try my hand. The result is not likely to rival your masterpieces but I promise that I will make it in fond though pale tribute to you.

Please take the best care of yourself. I am so grateful for all that you do for mamma and papa. We all love you dearly.

When you visit Timmy's grave, as I know you

will, with the first wildflowers of the year, place a few there for me.

———————

Dear Mamma,

I am having a leisurely morning. I've washed my hair and done a little mending (you can imagine how virtuous I feel knowing how I hate to take a needle in my hand) and am now awaiting Emily and Nels and two others who are joining me for lunch, so it provides a good opportunity to write these lines in certain knowledge that I'll not be interrupted for a while.

It was kind of you to let me know that papa does not disapprove of my interest in the Theosophical gatherings, and I do not resent his reinforcing your feeling that I should not become too involved and thus dissipate my energies or allow my undisciplined curiosity about mystical questions to lead me away from all that you have taught me.

I was not surprised that papa is not very impressed by the poetry I have sent to you. Nels tells me that in the past he has written rhymed verse, some in sonnet form, but he says it is all derivative and he refuses to show it to me, dismissing it as 'bad Byron' and 'synthetic Shelley'. Nels is totally in sympathy with the poetic canons of his group and is in frequent correspondence with Mr Ezra Pound. I'll send you a copy of the magazine con-

16

taining Nels' poem about me, but quite understand your feeling that you should not show it to our friends.

Yes, mamma, Nels seems increasingly attentive to me, but I hope you will not take it any more seriously than I do. I feel it is accurate to say that he is only attracted to the idea of being in love with me; that's how Emily put it, and I am inclined to agree. He has the romantic nature of his calling and responds eagerly to anyone who shows him sympathy. Like many of those in his group, he feels that the world is hostile to poets and this may account for his unreserved response to appreciation. Poor gentle Nels! I sometimes feel he lives more in his imagination and fantasy than in the real world. He is not religious; in fact, he claims to be an agnostic. Although there is a mystical streak in his nature it seems to be more a property of his intellect than of his soul. I think I am merely a catalyst to his Muse – surely a harmless relationship! – and that his poetry, even when he claims it is inspired by me, is not to be taken too seriously, for I feel it is impersonal. Emily dismisses his work as spectral and bloodless. She is an invigorating antidote to my sentimental tendencies . . .

———————

Paris
30 March 1909

Dearest Mamma,

. . . At the Stoughtons last evening we had a

17

fine time celebrating Emily's birthday. After dinner we gathered round the piano and sang songs, and then had an impromptu program, everyone being called upon to perform. I impersonated an overweight soprano of advanced years giving a kittenish rendition of 'ze *arietta*' created for her by 'ze great composer Hermann Hamburger' – quite off key, of course. Fortunately Prof Clémenceau was not present and was thus spared a few moments of agony. He appears to hold for me ambitions I do not myself aspire to, sometimes assigning me pieces which I feel will be forever beyond the range of any gift I have.

Emily's contribution was a series of impressions of people at an art gallery. Utterly hilarious! She is a born mimic and can assume accents and portray characters in a way that is amusing yet not unkind. Two of the best were the cockney charwoman who insisted on explaining to her incredulous companion chars that 'a painter is 'im wot paints'; and the socially-ambitious wife of the American *nouveau riche* button manufacturer ('My Casper's in buttons' she kept saying) who wanted to buy 'just a tiny oil – something that looks expensive and has a lot of peach to match my draperies and settee.' For an encore she impersonated her instructor conducting a life study class and defining a portrait as being a painting that purports to be a likeness of someone but which has something not quite right about the mouth.

Nels' offering was a comically-titled poem which he claimed to have written during dinner but which he later confessed he had commissioned another to compose, his Muse being rather too austere to engage in playfulness:

To Althea, between *hors-d'oeuvre*
and dessert

The loving things I long to say
You silence with: 'Have more *paté*?'

You turn to ash my private wish
By asking: 'Do you like the fish?'

Kisses on your lips I'd lavish,
But find you nibbling on a radish.

You turn to me your tender gaze
But ask: 'Please pass the *hollandaise*.'

I scarce descry my whereabouts,
And you exclaim: 'Such Brussels sprouts!'

My hand creeps out with sly intent;
You butter it by accident.

Would that my thought you might divine;
Instead, you say: 'Do try the wine!'

I sing to you: 'Tra-la! Tra-la!'
But you smile upon the rum-baba.

You pour my tea, yet give no balm –
Overfill my cup and scald my palm.

Our love is doomed to be platonic –
Your interest's plainly gastronomic.

And so it ran, verse after verse. Of course, everyone insisted that he write it out and all the guests signed it and it was presented to me with great ceremony. I was not untouched by Nels' effort to achieve, even by devious means, a light-heartedness that does not come readily to him. It was only a *little* unkind of the author to draw attention to my healthy appetite, but no doubt my unflagging interest in food will relieve Maggie's anxiety about my surviving among 'them foreigners that don't eat like us.'

Among the guests was a dark-haired young man, Michael Athlone, the author of Nels' poem. He has a disturbing air of mystery about him. His brooding manner and reticence I took to be, at first, sullenness, but I noticed that he followed Emily's banter with keen interest and flashed a great smile at her more outrageous jests. As the evening wore on he matched wits with her and joined us in singing some frivolous popular songs. I frequently felt him gazing at me intently and in silence as though he had it in mind to ask some profound question. I was flattered but somewhat disconcerted. I should like to know more about him though he seems self-contained and his extreme courtesy makes him appear distant and aloof. I know only that he was born in New York and spent his childhood in Montreal and Paris. He is associated with a publishing house here and seems to be well connected, yet not fully at ease with us.

We were reluctant to break up the party. We lingered till the early hours of the morning and then a group of us, still restless and too stimulated and happy to sleep, walked along the river as the sun rose. It was unusually warm and the sleeping city stretched out in rose and violet shadows as far as the eye could see. At one point Emily's pale hair was caught by a ray of light and she looked so ethereally beautiful that I ran forward and clasped her hand. I felt closer to her in that moment than I might to a sister and I longed for us to be together for ever. When I expressed the thought, she told me about a curious dream she'd had the night before: she and I were standing in a field of spring flowers with Nels and a few other friends, when a cream-robed figure appeared in the distance beckoning to us; the figure was indistinct but the countenance was shining. Emily and I, in the dream, were impelled to run toward the gleaming form but paused when we realized that the others had not moved. Emily called to them, urging them to join us, but they remained stationary, and she realized they could not *see* the figure. Together, then, we advanced, running pell-mell, hand in hand, irresistibly drawn by that beckoning hand. That was all.

I shivered when she told me. Mamma, I had had the same dream!

Paris
12 April 1909

Dearest Mamma,

I scarcely know where to begin, although the beginning should be easy to relate, so ordinary were the circumstances. One of Emily's friends who is active in Theosophical circles invited us to a reception for an American woman – well, that is

21

not quite accurate; she was born in New Jersey but now lives in Montreal – a Mrs Sutherland Maxwell. Her husband, I have learned, is a prominent architect. Learning that Mrs Maxwell had been invited to speak about her 'travels' I declined the invitation, in part because of my feeling that many people take journeys simply in order to be able to impress (or bore!) others with unending accounts of them – where they stayed and what they ate and how barbaric the natives were – but more exactly because I'd promised Nels I'd spend the evening with him. He's writing a long verse drama, the theme of which he has thus far kept a strict secret, but he asked me to hear him read the first act and I was hoping to have my curiosity satisfied. But at the last moment he took ill – one of those minor stomach upsets to which we Americans abroad seem so prone (I can hear Maggie saying 'I told you so!'). So Emily and I went and quite enjoyed the gathering in spite of our shared foreboding. At Emily's suggestion, Michael Athlone accompanied us. Any reluctance he might have felt he masked with his usual courtesy.

Mrs Maxwell spoke briefly about her visits to Palestine, portraying it as she first saw it ten years ago and as it is today, enchanting us with vivid descriptions of the land, its history and its people, and alluding to it as the physical and spiritual crossroads of the world's great religions. We were given far more than the 'travelogue' the hostess referred to in introducing the speaker; far more than the travel notes of a disinterested observer on the obligatory 'grand tour'. She spoke with an effortless fluid vitality that took us to the scenes she was describing; it was as though she were assisted by some invisible power, her face radiant and her eyes, at times, seeming to be fixed on a horizon not of this world. I could not accept it when she stopped to invite questions and the evening petered out in general conversation; I longed to shout 'Let's be silent and allow her to continue!'

It was impossible in the crowded room, during refreshments, to engage Mrs Maxwell in conversation privately, but when Emily and I approached to thank her, as we were leaving, it was as though she had sensed my thought. She clasped our hands in hers and said with great intensity that she'd like to see us again, her lovely eyes reflecting gravely the warmth of her words. I made a totally insincere protest – 'You will surely be very busy as a visitor,' etc. – but she cut across that dreary convention with words that went right to my heart: 'We are all visitors in this world and our time is brief; should we not search for truth while we may?'

I cannot imagine what caused Emily to say it but she blurted out my own unarticulated feeling: 'Then you *do* have more to tell us?' Mrs Maxwell replied, with a smile both mischievous and heavenly: 'I obliged my hostess. But, yes, my pearls, there is more and you shall have it all.'

How shall I fill the hours till we meet again next week? I am charged with a restless energy and with what I can only describe as a sense of dread, as though my life were about to take an unexpected course. How utterly charming and magnetic Mrs Maxwell is! We're to have tea with her next week, but meanwhile I am consumed with impatience, a shortcoming of mine with which I am sure you are only too familiar, dear.

Michael very kindly escorted us home but made little comment about the meeting and did not commit himself when Emily invited him to join us when we call on Mrs Maxwell next week. Emily continues to provide what I suppose is a desirable corrective to most of my effusions. Her usual response to my enthusiastic outburst on any subject is, 'We'll see.' She fights her own tendency to be swept away, shielding herself behind what I suspect is a manufactured scepticism. Even so I was not prepared for her next remark to Michael.

'I wouldn't miss next week's meeting for worlds,' she said. 'I must meet that woman again if only to learn her secret and prove it false.'

Even though Emily smiled, my heart shrivelled.

'Do you think Mrs Maxwell is a charlatan?' I asked.

'She may be – so many are,' Emily replied.

'Why must you always look for flaws in everything?' I protested.

'I'm a coward,' Emily said. 'Suppose one came upon unflawed perfection? Have you thought of the consequences? I feel ill-equipped to deal with the commitment that would be summoned, or the pain and ecstasy that might follow.'

'Do you think that may be what Mrs Maxwell is offering us?' I ventured.

'We'll see about that,' Emily said, and left us with a listless wave.

Mamma, grateful as I am for Emily's note of caution, I cannot contain my excitement nor rid myself of the conviction that Mrs Maxwell *knows* something, or is in touch with – shall I call it a power? – that can change all it touches. But if that is true, and pain and ecstasy are the cost, I hope I shall have the courage to pay the price willingly. Pray for me, dear.

————

Paris
15 April 1909

Dear Ada and Paul,

I have neglected you terribly, but know that mamma reads my letters to you when you come for Sunday dinner, and this eases my conscience somewhat. Paul deserves a better sister than I can ever be – (Ada, he truly was a very good brother, not patronizing me unduly, in the way of brothers who gaze down from the Olympian height of a three-year head-start in the nursery, and never teasing or bullying.) I have always felt I might be more worthy of the bounty of having been treated so well if I could have learned to recite by heart the eleven-times table or remember where 'N' comes in the alphabet without having to backtrack to 'L' in order to get the sequence right. Perhaps if I become a famous *prima donna* with Europe at my feet I shall make him proud of me and he will not consider that his patience with my limitations has gone entirely unrewarded. Think of the complimentary tickets for the royal box I could shower on him!

I hope you are both well and that the children remember their aunt whose love for them is not diminished by the miles that separate her from them. I have found a really remarkable doll for Bethany – she has her own little trunk with two changes of costume, complete with matching shoes and a tiny fur muff – and a splendid marionette for Roland, a wicked pirate with cutlass and an eye-patch. I enjoy speculating about the escapades Roland will lead him into.

Please send me your news. Mamma's letters, I fear, are edited by her kindness and her concern not to alarm or distract me. Papa's heart is not strong and he drives himself beyond reasonable limits in his service to his congregation. I shall count on you to keep me informed about those matters concerning which mamma is evasive. (You must not let her know that I have involved you in this espionage.)

You have my news, but shall I give you news of greater moment? Paul Poiret reigns as undisputed king among the more fashionable ladies of Paris. This season he bids us to adopt the look of little boys – his models are terribly extreme. I have given the matter serious thought and have concluded that I am anatomically disqualified from making the attempt. So I defiantly wear my green wool and tell my reflection in the glass how becoming it is to one of my coloring. A new hat and gloves, I have convinced myself, rescue me from being dismissed with the dowdy or identified with the vulgar. I'd pass inspection in Boston where our sartorial imaginations are kept in respectable check. Is it the weather that conspires to do so or our Puritan heritage?

A hug for the children, and fond love to all.

Dear Mamma,

I can scarcely find words to express my
disappointment. I wrote to you about our
appointment to meet Mrs Maxwell, an event to
which Emily and I had looked forward with such
excitement, but the result was curiously flat –
through our fault, I fear.

When we called on her she was obviously
unwell and we remained for something under an
hour. It was indeed extremely kind of her to
receive us at all. It was apparent that she had risen
with effort to meet us. Her lovely, youthful face
showed evidence of strain, and I realized that
although I had thought of her as a young woman,
she must be about forty, and has suffered all her
life from poor health.

I don't know what I was expecting of her – a
declamation of some kind, I suppose – but it was
all very ordinary. Mrs Maxwell led the conversation into very mundane channels, asking us
to tell her about ourselves, and creating an atmosphere in which it was easy – even inevitable – that
Emily and I should chat on and on, pouring out
our hearts. Whatever reservations Emily had
seemed to evaporate and I suppose I had none. I
was astonished to find myself telling her about

27

Nels and his theories of literature, how he feels that it can create a better social order out of chaos and hypocrisy, and even about my ambivalent feelings for him – that I dreaded his making an open declaration of love for fear I should be required to examine too closely the true station he occupies in my affections – and about the dream which Emily and I had had – things like that. And all of it without embarrassment. Mrs Maxwell has the most amazing capacity for – how shall I put it – receiving without disapprobation anything you offer, all the while surrounding you with an over-whelming sense of being loved. Each moment in her presence seems charged with a sense of sig-nificance. It is as if her whole being were infused by some radiant secret. Her brief comments, in a strange way, lent a unity to our otherwise spon-taneous babbling, relating everything we said to 'the spiritual purpose of existence.' With what curious authority she uses those words!

The point came when it would have been cruel to remain. She had sat like a gallant sponge absorbing with patient attention all we had said, but her fatigue became so obvious that it was imperative that we leave, though she did not even hint at it. I deplored the time we had wasted and apologized for having defeated our purpose in coming by prattling on and thus preventing our learning from her. She graciously thanked us for what *we* had taught her.

'But Emily and I want to be taught by you!' I exclaimed.

Her face was youthfully transfigured for a moment by her brightening smile. 'Well,' she said, 'perhaps we begin by learning that before offering the water of life to the thirsty, we must be sure his cup is empty.'

And so we left, unsatisfied but – well, 'uplifted' is the only word that comes to mind. And we are to meet again in three days.

Afterwards, I commented that Mrs Maxwell is like a polish that cleans the dross of workaday cares from the heart so that one feels mysteriously weightless and elated. I felt like a helpless fish caught in an invisible net from which escape is impossible and not the least desired.

'I learned so much from her,' I remarked to Emily when we were reflecting on our visit. 'Did you notice how sensitively she listened?'

Emily had, of course. One of the delights of our friendship is that we invariably notice the same things. But when I asked her later whether Mrs Maxwell had convinced her of her sincerity, Emily said, 'I'm convinced that she is sincere. But she may be sincerely wrong.'

'But have you ever felt such love!' I cried.

'Love is not enough,' Emily replied. 'There must be knowledge.'

'Perhaps next time she'll tell us her secret,' I offered.

'Her secret may be that she has no secret,' Emily said roguishly. But her excitement is no less than mine.

Emily's sharpest comments, I think, are her attempt to ward off disappointment. She once told me that happiness, like the sun, must be cautiously approached and with only sidelong glances.

I would choose blindness, mamma. And so, I believe, would Emily, despite her protestations.

———————

Paris
24 April 1909

Dear Nels,

Your note was delivered this morning and I am replying at once to say how sorry I am that we quarreled so pointlessly last night. It grieves me to think that I have hurt you, for your friendship means a great deal to me. Forgive my careless tongue.

Of course I want to see you again, for I am not willing to allow our friendship to suffer from a pointless misunderstanding. I truly did not mean to suggest that I find your play trivial – I simply do not *understand* it. Perhaps your bitterness will soften to the extent of allowing me to hear it again.

It was unfair of me to allow you to read it when I am in such an agitated condition, but there is a reason for that. You were right in remarking that I have not been myself lately; I shall be glad of the opportunity to attempt to explain. In any case, if our friendship should end I would seek a chance to thank you for all the kindness you have shown me.

The poem enclosed with your letter is beautiful, and I admire the delicate images. I loved the lines:

  . . . the silver mesh ensnares

the willing fingerling.
What hand draws the skein,
unseen, unseen?
Where no wave breaks,
where all is still,
one smiles in silence . . .

Oh Nels, you cannot know what those words mean to me!

Paris
26 April 1909

Dear Mamma,

Emily and I chuckled heartily over the message from Maggie which you relayed in your postscript, and we bow to the wisdom of her warning about 'them Frenchies and their flighty ways' and the 'new-fangled notions' that beset innocents on the Continent. I am continually amazed at her assessment of a world she has seen so little of, and unfailingly touched by her concern for anyone who has entered the compass of her affections. Tell her that I shall write to her soon.

The past weeks have been like a waking dream dominated by the presence of Mrs Maxwell – she has invited us to call her 'May' – and the series of meetings Emily and I have had with her. Although I wrote of meetings, May speaks of them more accurately as lessons. Their theme pierces my heart with poignancy. Mamma, she speaks of the return to earth of the Spirit of Christ to call an unheeding humanity back to God. Each time we have met we have been given more until my mind and heart have been flooded with a tumultuous joy and a deepening certainty as to the truth of her words. I long to hear more and more, but May replies gently that the veils which curtain us from truth should not be torn away brusquely, and thus we proceed at a measured pace. I see the wisdom of this – would not the total revelation of truth blind as the sun, or strike one dumb? – and yet I long for more! And this in spite of the fact that I am barely able to assimilate a single lesson – it all seems too dazzling, too incomprehensible for my understanding, too large for my mind to grasp. But I feel that I have waited all my life to hear these words. Can it be true that the Divine Spirit is with us again?

Emily and I try to speak of this when we are alone, but it seems to be a matter beyond the necessity of words. Often we lapse into a happy silence, or one of us will read a prayer given to us by May. Once when the three of us were together, May asked me to sing 'I am Thy Witness, Lord' and half-way through I burst into tears – it was the expression of joy on May's face and the fact that Emily was sobbing silently. Emily's doubts have melted; indeed she seems to have forgotten that she entertained them. She was dismayed to learn that Nels had an interview with Mrs Maxwell and found her an 'admirable but misguided' woman. 'Only someone made of wood and stone could resist May,' Emily exclaimed. Michael, too, has called on May but gently evades discussing his reaction beyond remarking that he found her charming and remarkable. Strange that Emily and I should want everyone to feel what we are feeling, and to know and love May as we do.

I startled Emily after one meeting by saying that her capitulation seemed to be an accomplished fact.

'Don't tease me about this,' she cried. 'I'm frightened.'

'Of ecstasy?' I asked.

'No,' she said, 'of the responsibility that flows from it. May told us that one cannot say "I believe" and not be tested. One must capitulate with every breath, deepen one's commitment to truth; divine salvation is not won by the simple declaration of belief.'

When I told Emily that I have every confidence that she will pass her tests with full marks she hushed me with her characteristic 'We'll see.'

I wish I had the same measure of confidence in my own capacity to meet tests successfully that I have in Emily's! Please pray for my strengthening.

————————

Paris
2 May 1909

Dear Paul and Ada,

I am so grateful that you let me know the full truth about the seriousness of papa's attack, for dear mamma, in an effort to spare me, only hinted at it. It is a comfort to know that you are close at hand should mamma need you, and Ada's training in nursing will add weight to her advice

33

to papa about avoiding stress. Thank heaven he consented to move his bedroom to the lower floor, for climbing the stairs would surely be an unnecessary strain on his heart. I'll be most circumspect in writing to mamma, for she would, I agree, be distressed to know that you had given me such detail. It has always been mamma's way to proceed by indirection and to protect herself and others from unpleasantness in the fond hope that it will simply disappear.

I am not *yet* in need of a trousseau, Ada dear. I find Nels very attractive but we have not spoken of marriage. I sometimes feel like a sister to him, sometimes like a mother; and he has some romantic and idealized image of me which I long to clear away so that he might see me as I really am. Then he might know whether or not he loves me and I might, at last, allow myself to consider whether I love him. I sometimes think I am capable of being consumed by love for him if only I were sure it were right.

I miss Emily very much since her return to Boston; it came about with a suddenness that left me reeling. I miss her more than I can say. When she has disposed of the house and settled her mother's affairs, she and her father are moving to New York to be closer to his family. Our friend, Mrs Maxwell, has given her letters of introduction to sympathetic friends there. Emily has promised to call on you and will, of course, see mamma and papa before she leaves Boston. It is a difficult time for her, for she was not close to her mother and her untimely death brings, in addition to a natural degree of sorrow, a burden of guilt, for she had

34

hoped to bring her mother closer. I am sure you will enjoy Emily – she has a sweet nature and, in usual circumstances, a ready wit. Above all, it is my ardent hope that she may allay your concern that Mrs Maxwell's influence may lead me to make unfortunate decisions. I am sure that mamma has confided in you her anxiety about this and I am hopeful that Emily will be able to ease her mind. If you knew how happy I am, you would not entertain a doubt concerning my welfare.

You will be glad to know that my studies are going well. Prof Clémenceau says my voice is improving steadily and while I should not rest on my laurels I may be permitted to register some slight degree of self-satisfaction; but then I must dismiss it at once, he says, for self-satisfaction is the mortal enemy of the artist.

Through Mrs Maxwell I have met a lovely circle of congenial people in the Bahá'í group – Emily will describe them to you when she calls. Edith de Bons has been wonderfully kind in introducing me to her friends who are interested in music. Mme de Bons has trained under Massenet and Cavallo and has a beautiful voice. I find myself attracted, too, to Laura Clifford Barney, an American who has lived here for a number of years and who gives me entrée to stimulating and artistic elements in the American colony. She guides me through the mysteries of the French culture and assists me with the language. My French gestures improve more rapidly than my pronunciation and vocabulary, but I find myself sometimes even thinking in French, so I gather hope. You must ask Emily to entertain you with her repertoire of Gallic gesticulations and her impersonation of a harassed concierge.

I await further word about papa and again express appreciation of your kindness in writing.

Paris
23 June 1909

My dear and so-dear-missed Emily,

I thank you for making such a concerted effort to win the approval of my family for the course we are taking. I know they would not fail to love you for your own dear self, and would listen to whatever you might say, for love of me. But how can we be sure they *heard* you! Your letter gave me little hope; still, I shall continue to pray that some seed of understanding will take root. Bless you for taking the trouble to call on them so faithfully during your own period of difficulty.

How wonderful that you and I should have been together, your last evening in Paris, when we wrote to the Beloved confirming our love and devotion to His Father's blessed Cause, and that our spiritual mother should have been witness to our covenant. May says that it is likely that 'Abdu'l-Bahá will write to us. The moment you receive your Tablet, please send me a copy of the translation, and I shall do likewise. Shall we one day enter the Beloved's presence together? I pray it may be so.

Our dear May, I am happy to say, is well, and tireless in her efforts to spread the Glad Tidings. My eyes mist when I think of her early days in Paris when alone and unaided she planted in the heart of Europe the precious Teachings she carried from 'Akká. The station of 'the first' must be very great. And the stories she tells of those days! I shall make notes when I can and send them to you, for I know you will cherish them as you do her letters. But this you must have at once. Remember our wondering why she called us her pearls? When I asked her about it she answered, as she so often does, in the Master's words. One pearl, He told her, is preferable to a thousand wildernesses of sand, and the pearl of great price is endowed with manifold blessings.

We who have been taught by May love her, but can we really know her value? Can we even imagine the joy she has brought her Master? The first 'pearl' of Europe, and now of Canada. What a blessing to have been associated with her and awakened to this Message. As our physical world grows smaller through the expansion and ease of travel and communication, will not such exploits become rarer and grow ever more precious? Perhaps we'll come closer to understanding their full significance in the future when there exist diminished challenges against which to test our heroism.

Are you painting? I want to know *all*. And who is this 'Peter' you mention so slyly in passing?

Nels is busy completing his play and Amy Summerville, an American poet who has recently come to Paris, has promised to read it. Her

37

approval seems important to him. She has prominent friends in American literary and publishing circles. She presents a rather theatrical and exotic appearance and would tempt you to caricature. Michael is respectful but elaborately courteous to her which causes me to think he is not impressed by her literary reputation.

Permit me to introduce the estimable Amy. Her poem 'Floodtide' appears in the current issue of *Focus*:

> I am the stone goddess.
> I stand alone in the desert
> in the burning noon
> brooding in heavy solitude,
> the hawk at my head,
> the serpent at my feet.
> Do not approach this wilderness.
> Should I break my silence,
> civilizations would drown
> in the torrent of my speech.

Occasionally I've had the misfortune to inadvertently blunder into her wilderness. I suppose the remedy would be to carry a compass. Failing that, perhaps I should learn to swim.

———

Paris
1 July 1909

Dearest Emily,

I am thrilled by your news of the Bahá'í friends in New York and it is especially rewarding to know that Berthalin Luxow had been a student in Paris and had known May! So you have found another sister. What a wonderful network of love has been woven about us by this Cause! I shall be grateful for any transcriptions of Tablets you are willing to send to me, for the words of the Beloved are the very breath of life, and you may be sure I'll share them with the friends here.

I am often speechless in our gatherings, so united is the group. I simply bask in the radiance, longing to have you here to be part of it, yet aware that we are linked by a bond that cannot be severed. I think of our little groups as candles, or perhaps as lighthouses, growing in number as the Teachings spread from mouth to mouth and heart to heart. Surely one day the world which so needs this light will be drawn to its beauty as its effulgence penetrates through the dismal gloom to the remotest corners of the globe. O darling Emily! To think that we are privileged to *know* in these earliest days! Now I want to perfect my voice; now I have a reason to sing!

Nels is in London where he feels he might interest a theatre group in producing his 'Fragments from the Greek.' Amy Summerville was enthusiastic about it and this bolstered his confidence. He has great faith in his play but the least discouragement about any of his work plunges him into a black depression. One of his nature does not have an easy time. We often quarrel of late over the most trifling matters, and one ill-chosen word of mine will cast him into despondency. And yet he has the same power over me. I wept the day I took him round to meet

May for a second time and he told me once again that he found her only 'a pleasant woman.' He accuses me of a frivolity of mind and says I chase immature idealistic fantasies in an effort to elude him. Our points of view are so different that I sometimes despair of our remaining friends. He says he loves me and I think he really believes it; but I fear he loves a 'me' his imagination or need has created.

And what do I need? I need *you* here to keep my sense of balance. Emotions are so untrustworthy and I detest the inner turmoil they cause. As I come to understand the Teachings more fully perhaps they shall be my balance. I suppose what I am really saying is that I miss Nels, too.

Prof Clémenceau surprised me yesterday by interrupting the lesson and saying, 'Mozart! Devote attention to Mozart! You must come to understand the daemonic.' One dares not ask the Oracle for explanations so I am left to mull it over on my own. I feel very much on my own without you here.

Amy Summerville – all flashing scarves and dramatic gestures – shows no inclination to be friendly. One night when a group of us were dining it was pointed out to her that I am a Bahá'í. She sighed theatrically, ensuring that every eye was fixed upon her, and said, 'My dear, faith died a long time ago. Its obituary was written belatedly by Matthew Arnold. He called it "Dover Beach".'

I tore my bread with unusual vehemence but held my peace.

Then directing her words to Nels, she said, 'It's charming to meet someone who cherishes the illusion that human beings are worthy of being salvaged.'

Surprisingly, Michael silenced her. 'And charming to meet someone who considers that a worthy observation,' he said, and then swiftly led the conversation to safe ground.

Paris
12 July 1909

Dearest Mamma,

It was happy news that papa is feeling stronger and I know you will, in your gentle and endearing way, continue to encourage him to exercise restraint. Maggie, I am sure, will support you in this effort with her unique brand of affectionate bullying. Is there no hope that you will be able to persuade papa to accept a smaller and less demanding parish? After so many years of devoted service to St. Martin's the congregation would miss him, but surely his responsibility towards his own health is also a spiritual obligation? I know papa is governed by the highest motives in all he does but I fear that he would view as a spiritual delinquency the slightest relaxation of his stern sense of duty and thus will continue to drive himself beyond his strength.

I have copied out for you a prayer which I say each day for you both; it brings you very close in mind and spirit. It is taken from a Tablet I received recently from 'Abdu'l-Bahá and speaks so beautifully of the healing power of the Word of

41

God that I hoped you might derive comfort from reading it, too. I have sent a copy to Ada, as well, for the loss of the baby in the third month of her pregnancy must have broken her heart. I could hardly bear to finish reading Paul's letter. Between the dry tone he employs to convey news of import I could hear the throb of anguish.

Emily is well and has had several portraits commissioned. One client complained that her technique was rather too forthright for the portrait to be totally satisfactory, but he seemed to feel that that was a risk one took in engaging an artist who charged such a modest fee. Emily commented in her letter that it might be interesting to increase her charges and offer the sitter the choice of being represented as a statesman (by exaggerating the brow to noble proportions as an indication of intelligence) or as an actor (by supplying an impressive profile and placing the sitter in a pose such as might be assumed by one delivering a soliloquy). 'You will note my wry smile,' she continued, 'as I ask myself why the human race has such a curious resistance to truth!'

Mrs Maxwell is returning to Montreal at the end of the month and I dread the thought of the separation. How I wish that you might meet her one day.

Edith Sanderson and I saw Diaghilev's Russian troupe the other evening. Never have I seen such dancing! Wonderful vitality. Nijinsky is the talk of Paris. He reminded me of a great doomed bird straining to fly toward a goal for which his wings were inadequate; the very air and light seem to support him as he leaps about the stage in an anguished ecstasy. At times he seemed poised between this world and some unseen realm which irresistibly compelled him. He strains against the natural laws which govern elevation as a bird might beat against the bars of its cage. Our applause appeared to startle him, as though we had surprised him at his devotions; as though his response to the music was a private affair not intended for the eyes of others.

Paris
18 July 1909

Emily, my dear,

Today Hippolyte Dreyfus presented me with a copy of his *Essai sur le Baháisme* which has just come from the printer, and I placed it on the shelf where it stands in dignity beside dear Laura's wonderful collection of the Master's table talks which so delighted the friends when it appeared last year in London. Slowly our little library grows. But I am impatient for the day when our books overflow the shelves and fill huge rooms and cause the foundations of great public libraries to creak and strain under the weight of countless tomes and the power of the Message in their pages. Oh Emily, I do not have a temperament suited to *beginnings*! I could not have come here empty-handed, as May did in 1899, with nothing to sustain her but the Tablet of her own crystal-clear heart on which the Master had inscribed

'Mine!' She was Bahá'u'lláh's first testimony in France; the first letter of all the books that will come from our pens here; the sole evidence of the power of the Creative Word on this continent. How can we and the world repay her?

Mamma wrote me to ask if I were faithful in my devotions and in response I sent her a copy of Mrs Waite's *Bahá'í Hymns of Peace and Praise* and a few prayers – some from the Tablets I received from the Beloved – hoping that she might ·feel an attraction to the spirit they express, but her reply was somewhat stilted and excessively polite, causing me to feel that she nurtures unexpressed doubts about my belief in Christ. If only she could see that my acceptance of the Promised One is the fulfillment of my every childhood prayer. I remember as a young girl sobbing uncontrollably when mamma read to me about the crucifixion of Jesus, and for weeks I asked her repeatedly if I would ever see and know our Lord. How ironic that I learned from my parents to pray 'Thy Kingdom come . . . ' and now that my deepest longing has been fulfilled and my heart has been flooded with happiness, mamma is secretly distressed. I say secretly, because it is not in her nature to express openly any thought which might cause a rift or unpleasantness. Perhaps she does not even discuss her concern with papa to avoid upsetting him. She may conceal from him, as well, the full truth of what I have written her. Perhaps I should not have said so much so soon.

I gather some of this from what mamma does *not* say in her letters. Maggie, the pivot of our household, continues to write counselling against

the dangers of living amongst 'them foreigners.'
She is a dear, pure-hearted soul and I am always
very careful to answer her respectfully. When
Maggie doesn't write, mamma very conscien-
tiously relays Maggie's cautions for her – as
though in Maggie's voice – and yet I feel Maggie
expresses in her direct and simple way the very
fears that hold sway over mamma's mind and
heart, fears which mamma doesn't dare express
on her own behalf. It is as though mamma were
frightened of seeing those things written out in
her own hand because she would then be required
to acknowledge the existence and extent of her
misgivings.

I must be kind to mamma so that I may avoid
placing her in the position of having to order me
to come home; and I must never allow myself to
say to my parents that it was their very own
prayers for me that opened my heart to seek and
accept the Light of the World. How glad I am that
your father is so tolerant and allows you to receive
the friends in your home.

Later: I return to you, Emily dear, after an
interruption, and rereading what I have written I
confess that I feel guilty for having expressed
what must seem like criticism of mamma, and
what must be a certain degree of self-recognition.
Am I not my mother's daughter? In the same way
as mamma, I shrink from facing the question of
whether I love Nels, and from knowing how he
really feels about the Cause, for then I might lose
him. I have not forgotten what May said, that we
cannot divide our lives, and it is to the inner life of
the Cause that every outer thing and circumstance

must adjust itself. I so readily see that faculty in May – it cannot escape notice, for she wears the love of God like a crown! – but it seems an unattainable goal for me. I cannot yet see how Nels would fit into the life I may one day be equipped to live, when I no longer feel torn between two worlds; when I have placed the Cause at the essential core of my life. That, I think, is the further shore toward which we must struggle. How clearly May reveals to the heart its own home! Strange, is it not, that I do not find myself wondering how I might adjust myself to Nels' life?

Nels writes from London that production of his play is a growing possibility, but the producer insists on inserting some modern dance sequences to be choreographed by a devotee and imitator of Isadora Duncan whose influence there is still being felt. Nels is concerned that this will weaken the dramatic effect of the speaking chorus and detract from the pace of the play. Apparently there is squabbling on Olympus. And since he is an unknown, and financing is a major issue – well, you can imagine. Having gone to them hat in hand, he can raise only mild objection. It all sounds so tedious and I am impatient with it, yet I do not want to see him hurt.

Did I mention that Amy Summerville is in London with Nels? She still intimidates me a little – her outsize gestures, her eclectic costumes, the cigarette holder she brandishes. She likes to advertise herself as a 'Divorced Person' – her tone capitalizing the words and hinting at a dark scandal. I've never before met someone who

was divorced, I told Michael. My parochial upbringing has limited my exposure to people who
are very different from myself; divorced persons
just didn't find their way into the family parlor.
Michael seemed suddenly vexed. 'People are what
they are,' he snapped. 'They have to make the best
of it and so do we.'

I was shocked by his vehemence and felt very
gauche.

'Now that you're a Bahá'í,' he continued, 'it's
time you stepped out of the parson's parlor into
the world and met the teeming masses – Moslems,
Jews, Hindus, saints and sinners, freethinkers,
divorced people. Not everyone has had the
advantage of being a minister's daughter.'

I was angry at being misinterpreted by Michael,
and puzzled by having upset him. Do you
suppose he is divorced? But I have resolved to be
less frightened of Amy so that I may be free to like
her more. I truly admire her élan and the courage
with which she conducts her somewhat hap-
hazard life, as though she makes it up as she goes
along, and has no fixed reference points – except
perhaps herself; she is at the center of the small
dramas she creates about her.

I am wondering what it is about me that
sometimes causes Michael's courteous composure
to break? Once when I thought he was being
unfair in his assessment of a poem Nels had written
I pointed out that suffering might have given it
birth. Michael, who was being discursive, colored
suddenly and said with unusual force, 'Nels is far
from even identifying his vague discontents.
Suffering can spring from many sources but it

means little unless it is faced heroically and triumphed over.'

'I always associate heroism with joy,' I said. I was thinking of the martyrs.

'I, too,' said Michael. 'I sometimes think there's so little joy in the world because there are so few heroes. Everyone in the small domestic circumstances of his life can be a hero. But we lack the passion heroism calls for and instead become models of mediocrity, smug and safe and cowardly.'

I hoped he might continue but he lapsed into silence and when he spoke again it was with that regrettable courteousness that seals him in as effectively as a suit of armor.

Paris
3 August 1909

Dear Emily,

Prof Clémenceau's mustache had occasion to twitch especially vigorously this morning and he interrupted my dissonant and dispirited efforts by saying, 'My dear Miss Benedict, let us cancel the lesson today, for we cannot continue when you are croaking like a lovelorn frog. Shall we try again tomorrow?' But his eyes twinkled as he said it, and I realized that he was attempting to be cheerful and kind. He knows that May has left Paris and perhaps guesses or has been told what it means to me, how keenly I feel the loss.

All the friends are trying to cheer one another

but we do not have the resources; we have all lost our mother, our sister and our friend. One of the Persian friends gave me a small dried flower which a relative had sent to him from the resting place of Bahá'u'lláh and said, 'Take comfort in this sweetness.' The tender gesture touched me and I found myself thinking what a wonderful place the world will be when all develop towards one another this sensitivity, this gift of reading the needs of the heart. May's last words to us, as you might expect, were words she heard from the Master's own lips: 'Separation is only of our bodies; in spirit we are united.' I find consolation in this thought and try to imagine how our own experience of grief must be but the palest hint of the weight of grief of the Holy Ones.

Although I am not yet reconciled to May's departure I rejoice that we will carry on the Great Work here, even as she returns to take up the task in Quebec. Service, I feel, is the only anodyne. The work must go forward for the world needs this Message very much and the workers are so few. I sometimes feel that time is running out for me – perhaps for us all – and there is so much to be done. When will Greenland be conquered in His Name? Who will subjugate Africa to the Divine Will? When will the Light be carried to the Antipodes? We are a handful and the fields stretch out before us seemingly without end. When I think of what must be done I long to snatch my heart from out my breast, dash it into a million pieces and scatter its shards across the universe so that no corner of the earth may be deprived of at least some small glimpse of the radiance of this

New Day. And yet my heart is so inadequate to reflect this effulgence, and my will flags. Oh Emily, pray that I may become a worthy mirror.

What are you reading these days? Please send me some recommendations. Michael has put me on a diet of Henry James for whom he has considerable admiration and I yearn for some variety. Please recommend nothing relentlessly serious; I crave literary bon-bons, pastries and creams. If I really sought to impress you I'd list the books I have been reading in French!

Paris
28 August 1909

My dear Ada,

How kind of you, in the depths of your mourning, to let me know that the prayer that I sent to you brings you solace and that you have committed it to memory. Yes, truly, the words are, as you say, 'as if written by one not of this world.' I shall enclose some other passages from that same pen in the hope that you will derive comfort and benefit from them. About their author, I have much to tell you if you would care to know one day, for his life is a source of inspiration to all who meet him and his words bring fulfilment of their hearts' desire. I have just spent the afternoon with one who came from his presence, and so radiant was the pilgrim's countenance that it was as though I could reach out my hands to her face and have them warmed as if by a fire. 'To meet our Master,' she said, 'is to find courage to begin the schooling of the soul in the divine discipline of personal transformation.'

I am happy that Paul and the children are well and that Paul continues to enjoy his work at the bank. His promotion was surely well deserved for I know he devotes himself wholeheartedly to his occupation. He is like papa in that respect. I have always been slightly in awe of Paul, not only because he is my brother and as a young boy exacted from me all the respect due an older sibling, but because he displayed from the earliest years a singleness of purpose and a gift for organization that made me feel vaguely wanton! I recall that he kept an accurate written record of the number and color of his marbles, and a tally of how many he lost or won in each game. The contents of his bureau drawers were always impeccably arranged while mine were helter-skelter. I predicted long ago that if he did not follow papa into the church he would have a successful career as an accountant or manager.

I am always grateful for the news you give me of mamma and papa, for I am never sure that mamma, with her penchant for euphemism, is not shielding me from worry, and of course I want to know in detail whatever is to be known.

Maggie wrote telling me that you were 'an angel' when papa had 'that bit of a bad turn.' I am grateful to you, Ada dear, ever and always, and knew, long before Maggie's declaration, that you are indeed an angel.

I am learning a few songs by Debussy, beautiful and winged creations with which I feel very much at ease.

Paris
12 September 1909

Dear Nels,

I was thrilled by the news! I wish I could accept your invitation to the opening, but it is simply not possible for me to come to London, much as I would like to. Emily, I am sure, would love to be there, too. All the Bahá'í friends here send you their warmest greetings and have asked me to express their good wishes for the success of the play. We are all happy to think that if all goes well you may be back here soon for a visit. There will be rejoicing in the cafés! To have been separated from Emily, May and you in quick succession has been a greater exercise in detachment than I was prepared to meet.

I have not seen Michael Athlone recently but the last time we spoke he mentioned that there was considerable dissension among the writers' group about what direction they should be taking. Several have withdrawn and established a new clique. He spoke most disparagingly of Mr Pound and his ideas, and said it is time for all poets to reassess their values. The new group is working on an anthology, as you perhaps know.

You ask whether I am still interested in the Bahá'í Teachings. Nels, I find that question most difficult to answer in a letter without laying a foundation so that my emphatic 'Yes!' might be better understood. If I am sincere and acknowledge that for me these Teachings are true and represent the very spirit of this age, then you will understand that I cannot be merely 'interested' but must be committed. The quest for truth is not something one takes up occasionally, like knitting. After all we have said, how can you think it would be so with me? I'm sorry that I express it so poorly. When you return to Paris I shall try to explain. Please convey my good wishes to Amy.

Paris
13 September 1909

Dear Nels,

I send this letter close on the heels of the one I sent yesterday. Perhaps it is wrong of me to attempt to say in a letter what I feel I could say better face to face, but I slept poorly last night and my lesson today went badly – Prof Clémenceau said my voice was 'murky with doubt and strain' – and as a result I am feeling depressed. I miss you very much and wish you were here so that I might explain my 'interest' in the Bahá'í Teachings. I have brewed a large pot of tea and made a small fire to cheer myself up, but I really need to hear your voice and have you tell me that I am beautiful and gifted and destined to succeed – all blandishments would be wholeheartedly welcome.

Nels, I see it in such a simple light, perhaps because I am a simpleton. If there is a God and I have an immortal soul, then the relationship of my soul to God, its creator, is the most important thing in the world, and anything which does not advance that relationship is of lesser reality – I had almost written 'a waste of time'. Oh Nels, this

53

is pointless. This cannot be set out on paper discursively; I am foolish to make the attempt. I cannot give you faith. I cannot make you see or understand, no matter how much I might wish it for you. Words are the least part of faith; it is a gift to be lived, and I am a beginner in this life.

I'll not go on; I'll end up defending myself and earning your contempt. Let us, when we meet, try not to keep stumbling over the obstacle of words and opinions; let us try to find another way.

Does it help if I say that I do not know what the Bahá'í Faith is? I dimly glimpse that it is the only direction the world can safely take and, as such, I must give it my allegiance and let its impulse lead me where it will. I would presume to out-guess God if I were to say more.

Last night I dreamed I was giving a recital before a large and distinguished audience – somehow I knew that the great Jean de Reszke was present – and you were sitting in the royal box splendidly attired and in the company of a number of prominent, glittering people whom I could not identify. The curtain rose and there was a burst of applause; then my accompanist struck the opening chords of the first selection. I was suddenly horrified because I did not know the song, it was utterly new to me. I faltered a moment, and then began to sing – far more beautifully than it was ever possible for me to do; the music was unlike any I have ever heard, exquisite beyond description, and the words were supplied to me from some mysterious source – it was as though they were familiar. I filled the

54

theatre with light clear tones and felt flooded with power. The audience gave me a standing ovation, applauding tumultuously. When I looked up you were gone. Then, in the way of dreams, you appeared and looked at me accusingly and asked, 'Why did you flee from the stage when the music began?'

I protested that I had sung but you insisted that you had not heard me and turned away. I woke up feeling confused and bereft.

I am weary now, and must sleep. I think a head cold is coming on and I must prepare to do battle with it.

I breathlessly await news of the progress of your play which I hope will be a triumph.

Paris
16 September 1909

Dear Nels,

I won out against the cold! Whether it was prayer or the application of Maggie's remedy (an extraordinary concoction of lemon juice and spices) or sheer determination, I cannot say, but today I feel much better. This morning I composed a little verse which I feel emboldened to send to you; I hope you won't think it silly – I call it 'Rainbow':

> Surely it will not always be
> that we shall stand
> hand clasped in comforting hand
> in a grey and disadvantageous light

where the waves gnaw with white teeth
the infirm shore while above a lone gull
addresses its rusty protest
to the uncomprehending sky.
Not always will you ask timorously
what I see, terrified that I, too,
deny you the beneficent portent.
Until the delectable omen lodge there
make, then, your soft request; let me
furnish to your straining eye
the multicolored miracle.

If you find it necessary to criticize my poem, please be gentle. I sometimes compose little verses, and sometimes fit them to melodies, but am somewhat shy to show them. But I trust you not to ridicule me!

A cold spell has overtaken Paris and winter will soon be upon us. Let me know how the play is going and be assured of my best wishes for its success.

———

Paris
20 September 1909

Dear, dear May,

It was so lovely to find your welcome letter when I returned from Laura's and, as you might guess, we spoke of you. So vividly did your face come to mind in those moments that I had a distinct expectation that a letter would come. Its coming sooner suggests to me that my hunger speeded it. No day goes by but I think of this imperishable gift you have given me. It grows in luster and magnificence as time passes and my feeble understanding strains to embrace its reality. I have come to know how true are the words you so often spoke, describing the Cause of God as being like a great university from which we never graduate, an inexhaustible font of Divine knowledge.

The friends will be overjoyed when I share the news of the progress of the work in Canada. The love you inspired amongst us still binds our hearts and is ever fed by the pilgrims who pass through, their faces aglow with the awe of having been in our Beloved's presence. Recalling how you said we must not heed our frailty and weakness but must remember always that it is the Spirit of God that moves the work forward, I try to follow your example in waiting for the Spirit and doing what It bids, but too frequently my inadequacies rise up to daunt me. But slowly I learn. Sometimes I simply pray, 'I await; use me!' Perhaps that is my purest. prayer. When the confirmations come I weep privately in gratitude, often reminding myself of the Master's words to you: 'As your faith is, so shall your powers and your blessings be.'

I enclose my notes of an account one of the pilgrims related of the placing of the remains of the Báb in the mausoleum on Mount Carmel on Naw-Rúz day after sixty years during which that precious dust was concealed and transferred from place to place. How great the Master's joy must have been that He was able to carry out, at last, His Father's holy command. How dare I speak of anything I experience as being 'faith' in the light of the Master's example? The strange coincidence of the arrival in the Holy Land on that same day of the announcement that the friends in America have created the Bahá'í Temple Unity to hold title to the land where the Temple will be constructed has thrilled us; how much greater the significance of this must be to the Beloved Whose eyes are lifted to a horizon far beyond ours. O May! I pray that our hopes will be realized and that one day He may be among us here in Paris. I so yearn to see Him, but cannot yet see how it can be arranged for me to make my pilgrimage to the Holy Land. I shall broach the subject gently to my family, but I fear they will consider it a bizarre suggestion. The Master in Tablet after Tablet counsels me to show them submissiveness and love, and admonishes me to achieve a degree of patience far beyond my limited capacity – or so I feel! Perhaps one day my obedience to them will be the portal through which they will glimpse the Peerless Face.

Laura and Edith are well. Your name is frequently on our lips.

———

Paris
18 November 1909

Dear, dearer, dearest Emily,

I have received a most touching letter from my sister-in-law, Ada. Her gentle spirit seems attracted to the Teachings, and I shall be very grateful if you would consider calling on her

58

when you are next in Boston. The grief of losing her baby has turned her mind to the other world and she may be receptive. Will pain always be the necessary tiller of the heart's soil to prepare it for acceptance of Divine Seed?

I shall pave the way for you, of course, with a letter to Ada, but you may be sure of a warm reception, for she wrote after your first visit saying how much she admired your personality. That augurs well, for it is natural enough, I suppose, that one is attracted to the vessel and then the wine. I have sent her some prayers which she uses daily and these will surely have had an effect. Paul is somewhat austere, as you know, and she is always most careful not to offend him, so you will know what to do. My parents will also be glad to see you and will draw reassurance from your happy nature. Mamma wrote after your earlier visit that you were a 'delightfully lively and normal girl' and although that is less than I hoped for, it is a beginning. I wonder, though, whether she had expected you to be an exotic! Perhaps she fears our interest in what she still insists on calling 'Eastern philosophy' will lead to our wearing the costume of the harem, or a chádur. And if *that* puts any ideas in your impetuous and dearly-loved head, kindly confine them to your sketch pad!

Nels is as exasperating as ever. I foolishly wrote a long letter to him in which I tried to explain my feelings about – well, the purpose of life, and my faith in the truth of the Bahá'í Teachings, and all those things which really matter and concerning which words seem to be a hindrance to understanding – I received a note from him which made it clear that I failed utterly in conveying my meaning. I knew even as I was writing it that I should have awaited his return in order to talk to him about it, but vanity and irritation drove me on and I wrote and mailed it. Nels seems to see me still as pursuing childishly an unidentified Ideal (he won't accept that I have found and named it) and as refusing to recognize what he states is the 'urgent claim' he has on my affections. He doesn't ask that I abandon the Cause – he won't go so far as to admit to himself that I have found anything of worth. Instead, he asks me to choose him, rather than (his very words) choose the fruitless chase. He has dedicated another poem to me, and because it illustrates the attitude I just spoke of it saddens rather than flatters me:

> I would have you be
> moth to the candle
> my song ignites,
> but another light consumes you.
> What song is this
> and who the singer?

Of course, I remind myself that his play is about to be launched, and with rehearsals every day he is under considerable strain, so I shall not write immediately; or, rather, perhaps I shall, but only in the most general terms and on neutral subjects. He is always tense and prone to discouragement and I should not wish to say anything which might cause despondency. (One pays such a high price for sensitivity!) Later, when we are both calmer, I shall look for a way to say what is in my heart. Pray, Emily, that I shall never be forced to choose between *love* and *Love*.

———————

Paris
20 November 1909

Dear Mamma,

Again the Birthday of Jesus approaches and I am imagining how busy you are. I know how much you enjoy it but that does not prevent my urging you not to work beyond your strength. I think your idea of inviting Emily to join you for Christmas is most kind, and I am sure she will be delighted to accept if she can. Rest assured that I shall be with you in spirit, with Emily as my physical deputy. She has many friends in Boston and of course she would be happy to see Paul and Ada again. Let me know if you are able to arrange it. For my part, I shall write and urge her to accept.

Emily is hoping to come to Paris next year and has suggested that I accompany her to the Holy Land if we receive permission to proceed there. I would dearly love to do so, and wonder whether you and papa would give your consent? Perhaps you could discuss it when Emily is with you and she is able to tell you her plans. I cannot describe how I long to make the journey, nor have I words adequate to define the tumult that stirs my heart at the thought that I might one day glimpse my heart's desire.

Prof Clémenceau is urging me to attack the

Song Cycle 'Schéhérazade'. When I told him that an attack is probably what my efforts would amount to he smiled and said that Ravel's work had withstood assault from highly accomplished assassins and survived unscathed.

I attend Mozart concerts when the opportunities present themselves and am a little frightened by what Prof C. calls the daemonic which underlies the sublime. But perhaps to encompass these extremes is to embrace the totality of our human condition. There is something false about a spiritual life that denies being rooted in our animal existence, just as there is an ignoble distortion in a life that deprives us of winking back at the stars because our snouts are grubbing in the mire.

Thank you for letting me know that the gifts I mailed have arrived safely and that you will place them under the tree. I wish I could be there to see the children's eyes when you lead them to the lighted tree. Please give my love to all.

———————

Paris
3 January 1910

Dear Emily,

I am struggling very hard to remember to put '1910' on the letters I write today, for the New Year has for me, at first, the quality of strangeness; but in a week or so I shall accept it as I would a pair of worn and comfortable shoes.

You can well imagine how I await your next letter! I don't promise not to sleep until it comes, but at the moment I cannot conceive how I shall manage to do so. I shall want to know *all* about your visit to Boston.

A long silence followed my last letter to Nels and then a bulging envelope arrived and a note, 'Althea, I'm sorry'. Not another word. And enclosed was the explanation in the form of press reviews, one all the more insulting for the faintness of its praise, and the others unanimously condemning. These excerpts will tell you why I feel alarmed. One critic wrote:

'In "Fragments from the Greek" we were promised much and given little. Setting his play in an unidentified period of the much-abused history of ancient Greece, Mr Erikson sought to draw parallels between the conditions confronting the society of that time and those which he feels beset us in this day. He errs gravely in assuming his own melancholia to be a general condition . . .

'A chorus of whirling creatures clad in scandalously diaphanous robes added to the chaos by hurtling about the stage with admirable but undisciplined athleticism, considerably weakening the already faint dramatic line and generally disporting themselves in a manner more in keeping with the vulgarity of a music hall performance than befitting a serious theatrical production . . .

'If throughout the play the Oracle did not speak it could only be because words failed . . . '

Could it have been *that* bad? And another review must have been even more hurtful to Nels, for it attacks him rather than the vehicle:

'. . . his poetic manner is barely distinguishable from that of several of his contemporaries. He is handicapped by a narrowness of vision and

vocabulary, and in straining for mystical significance he reveals a fatuous pretentiousness. His
ambitious verse drama is a pastiche of precious-
ness which betrays him by its insincerity, its lack
of integrity and emotional depth, and its self-
conscious concern to be modern.

'Mr Erikson would seek to declare war on the
established literary conventions armed only with
a lace-edged handkerchief. His hackneyed theme
that noble art alone endures, outlasting the sceptre
and the citadel, has long since been expressed by
Masters of literature at whose unblemished feet
Mr Erikson should humbly cast himself, as
becomes an insolent student. There let him beg
forgiveness and gain mastery of his craft. To Mr
Erikson we say, treacle and bombast do not a poet
make – *poeta non fit sed nascitur . . .* '

My poor Nels! So filled with revolutionary
spirit and no adequate outlet for the heroism of
which I think him capable. I have no clue as to
where he is or what he will do, and no idea how I
can help him. I shall let you know as soon as I
hear, of course.

Michael, who had not seen the script, expressed
no surprise at Nels' treatment by the critics; not, I
learned, because he despises their function and
their frequent acrimony, but because he has no
faith in Nels' capacity to write a successful stage
piece. 'The man's character is against him, as well
as his youth,' he said. 'Lacking personal
integration and a unified vision or aesthetic, he
will write with a flashy excellence but is not likely
to be able to sustain it. I think his work would not
hold together.'

'But you must applaud his courage in trying,' I offered weakly, remembering my own ambiguous response to Nels' play.

'I do,' Michael replied, and added – I thought patronizingly – 'Just as I applaud yours in presenting him with a vision of a world united in faith, a concept which I think his imagination has not yet the power to accept.'

'But if I persist, he may come to accept it in time,' I said – inanely, I suppose, and somewhat prissily, for I was piqued.

'We'll see,' he concluded, and I almost smiled to hear him echo the words you habitually use to express reservation. 'Nels' lack of personal unity and his inability to grasp what you offer are related, of course.'

'Let's stop sitting in judgment of poor Nels,' I snapped. 'If he accepts the Bahá'í Teachings they may give him the inner harmony you say he lacks.'

'Why is it always "poor" Nels?' he asked.

'Stop it,' I cried. 'You've gone too far. Can't you sympathize with Nels in his failure?'

'Only too well, because I read in it the symptoms of my own,' Michael said and retreated behind an apology. Only later did I realize how rare it was to hear him speak so frankly. I shall take pains to apologize to him next time we meet. I thought today that Michael would be an ideal subject for Correggio's brush – stark and emphatic contrasts; small areas brilliantly illuminated, but much provocatively concealed in a dark ground of twilight that stubbornly resists yielding its secrets to the eye.

Lucrezia Bori is to appear here shortly with Caruso in *Manon Lescaut*, but my anxiety over Nels casts a bleak shadow upon my anticipation of that delectable fare. I conceal my worry from Laura and Hippolyte and Edith Sanderson who'll accompany me to the performance, as I do not wish to spoil their pleasure.

———————

Paris
10 February 1910

Dear Mrs Brittingham,

I have heard of the wonderful work you are doing in carrying the Glad Tidings wherever you go and wish to commend you wholeheartedly on the marvelous system of correspondence you have assisted in establishing between the Bahá'í women of America and their sisters in the communities of Persia. I shall be very happy to participate if you feel that reports of the activities of the friends here will gladden their meetings and strengthen the bonds that unite our hearts. In like manner the friends here were very inspired by your news that Mr and Mrs Alec Frankland of California have now settled in Mexico City and are informing interested seekers of the truth of the New Day.

We have heard, as perhaps you will have, too, of the splendid work that Dr Susan Moody is doing in Persia. Surely this beginning will pave the way for more of us to follow in her footsteps as circumstances permit, for we are told there is a great need for friends from the West to settle there and assist by teaching English and other subjects to the Bahá'í children. It is difficult for us to imagine the restrictions which govern the activities of the believers there, and particularly the difficulties their environment imposes upon our Eastern Bahá'í sisters.

One of the Persian friends told me how important it is for the friends in that land to see the believers from the West as proof of the power of Bahá'u'lláh to raise up servants to carry on the work for which so many of their kinsmen gave their lives. He spoke so movingly of the martyrs of Yazd who were so cruelly slaughtered in 1903 that I was in tears, and out of kindness he fell silent until I overcame my cowardice in listening to those heart-rending accounts, and gaining control insisted that he continue so that I might better understand the meaning of devotion and self-sacrifice. I cannot forget his description of the youth of eighteen who was denounced by his own father and handed to the mob which tore him to pieces before the eyes of his distressed mother who was holding aloft a copy of the Qur'án and pleading for the life of her beloved son.

We have so much to learn from the friends of the East! There is a subtle poetic quality in all they do, and their very conversation is a delicate art form. They gently lead along always aiming, though indirectly, at a fixed point which at first remains obscure but which is eventually revealed with a vivid force, leaving one with a peculiar sense of being an actual part of what is being related, so that not only one's mind but one's soul

67

is imprinted by the narrative. How unlike the Westerner who craves the direct result and demands to see the end in the beginning! So in listening to the account of the martyrs and realizing that these events occurred within my own lifetime, it was as though I had been transported there and was confronted with my own degree of faith, and the question: Would I die for this? And how to answer this, I ask myself, when I feel uncertain, as yet, how well I might live for it. To live it, of course, is our first task.

The friends in Paris are united and are deriving much joy from the sweet labor of raising the Divine Call. They join me in sending warmest greetings.

Paris
18 February 1910

Dear Emily,

We grow accustomed to our own despair and limitations and are always shocked when we realize that those we love or admire or envy or look up to have moments of doubt and self-dissatisfaction. Your letter saddens me only because you are so hard on yourself, and I cannot bear to know that you are blaming yourself for failing to win my parents' approval of our plan to make pilgrimage together. Let us leave it in God's hands, knowing that we have done all we can, and continue to pray for a solution. Meanwhile, you must proceed as though the success of the venture were assured. And whether or not I am able to accompany you to the Destination of Delight, we shall at least be together in Paris for a time.

Mamma has written that your conversations with her during the Christmas visit gave her much to think about, so do not feel that all is lost, for perhaps this means she will relent. As for Ada, she never has much to say, that dear and pensive mouse, so if she appeared to merely listen with wrapt attention you may be sure she registered what you said and will hold it in her heart. This is her way. And Maggie, that stern judge of character, has written to me about your visit. Your talks with her were far from a waste of breath, as you may conclude from her comment, as succinct and heartfelt as it is ungrammatical: 'Whatever the Bahá'í movement is, it isn't just nothing.' High praise from Maggie! Had you not touched an inner spring the depth of Maggie's contemptuous silence would have deafened you.

So do not berate yourself as an inadequate instrument. How can any of us be adequate to the Message we bear? Why else are we bidden to disregard our limitations and weaknesses? May stressed this so strongly in our conversations, long before I was able to apprehend the necessity for it. But it is true! The power of the Cause, it seems to me, lies in its ability to raise up imperfect instruments to carry out the perfect plan of God. *That* is the mystery; *that*, the miracle! I look at the pilgrims who pass through Paris and see them, when all is said and done, as very ordinary people; it is in their response to the Teachings that they are transformed, enabled to become, each in his own way, something far greater than he otherwise might have been. Their faces glow, their words enchant, but what one remembers of them is the spirit they reveal.

One pilgrim recently addressed us and I was deeply stirred while she was speaking. Later I realized it was not because of what she said – indeed her voice was almost unpleasantly nasal and distracting – but because of the stature of her belief which illumined the room. As she spoke she seemed a towering figure with a most commanding presence. Over refreshments, chatting about the difficulties of transportation abroad, I became conscious of a mole on her chin, fatigue lines about her eyes and a marked degree of shyness in her manner, and I wondered momentarily whether I had imagined her earlier power. No, I realized. She is neither a magician nor an actress, but an extraordinarily ordinary, humanly human, woman of the kind one would pass on the street without a glance. And with it I saw the miracle – she is a magnificent channel of the Spirit because she steps aside to let it work through her. If she thought of her physical limitations she would never open herself to be an instrument of the power of the Faith. What a loss, I thought. And what a tragedy if I were to cut myself off from that power by being aware only of the woman's somewhat grating voice, the mole, the evidence of fatigue. In that moment I loved her even more, for I felt I truly saw her essence.

But I am rambling on about 'seeing' to you who first taught me to see light and shadow, and within the shadow further light! Just let me say, though, that our lives, our deeds, like our words, may seem very ordinary and workaday, but it is the quality of service and love with which we invest the ordinary things we do which will, I think, touch the hearts and lead others to the Kingdom. Therefore, because you made a most ordinary visit to my parents at Christmas and did all the ordinary things one does in such situations, they cannot fail to have noted the spirit in which you went about it. Now, surely, *they* have some responsibility in the matter! Our task is to offer the gift with a pure heart and a correct motive and to detach ourselves from the response of the one to whom it is offered. I asked Hippolyte recently what he conceived to be the highest service a Bahá'í can render. I'm still chuckling over his reply: 'To always do the thing under his nose that needs doing.'

No word from Nels, but one of his poet friends reported seeing him in the Latin Quarter last week in a rather rowdy (possibly drunken) condition, but lost him in the crowd before having an opportunity to speak or to be really certain it was him. Distressing news, if it is true. I have sent notes to his former address in Paris but received no reply. I shall let you know when I hear further of him.

But enough of that. You must think of nothing now but your pilgrimage, knowing that if God wills it, I shall join you. But my possible inability to do so in no way diminishes my happiness that you are able to go. I am glad that your friend, Peter, has expressed such interest and delight in your going.

Now that the Beloved has transferred His residence to Haifa and is free, after the rigors of 'Akká, to stroll on the Mountain of God, the friends should find it possible to visit in increasing numbers. I am told the climate of Haifa is more salubrious than that of the Prison City, and that in spring the mountain is a carpet of wild flowers. How pleasant after the gloom of 'Akká!

Recently Edith and Joseph de Bons gathered us together to hear again their account of their pilgrimage. It was in 1906 but they made it seem like yesterday. Sometimes the Master would invite Edith to sing 'Holy City' on the terrace of the house in the evening so that He might hear her from His own room. Imagine having one's voice carried through the still air to the ears of One Who hears the music of the spheres.

I am overjoyed that publication of a Bahá'í magazine under Mr Windust's editorship is to become a reality next month. Yes, please do send me a copy as soon as it is available. I am so delighted that at last we will have a means of keeping abreast of the progress of the work around the world.

———

Paris
1 March 1910

Dear Maggie,

I was very pleased to receive your letter and delighted with the photograph you enclosed. You look wonderful in that black taffeta – or is it a dark blue? Very handsome, anyway. I have found a charming frame for the picture and it rests on my table with photos of mamma and papa, and Paul and Ada and the children, so that I may look up at any moment from my desk and catch in my vision the dear faces of those I love smiling at me. I am glad of *your* presence in this group because of that special degree of loving concern you have for all of us. Under your watchful eyes, of course, I shall now certainly make an extra effort to mind my P's and Q's.

You are dear to ask about my health. I take long walks and do some exercising with the result that I feel well and my figure is – well, if not that of a sylph, at least of lady-like proportions. Lillian Russell has made life difficult for us all! I take a secret satisfaction in reports that the sands are thickening in her hourglass.

Thank you for letting me know that papa's recent illness was nothing more than a mild influenza and not another attack. You should not now be troubled at the thought of visiting your brother in Nova Scotia, especially since your capable friend, Esther, has agreed to fill in for you.

No, dear Maggie, I have not seen Mr Erikson lately – I cannot adopt your phrase 'my young man', for he is scarcely that! But he has had difficulty recently and after the failure of his play he may be reluctant to face his friends. I have heard that he has returned to Paris and is working as a journalist. When he is in an improved frame of mind no doubt his old circle of friends will have the pleasure of his company once again.

Do have a good visit with your brother and be assured that I shall pray for you each day, as you do for me.

———————

My dear Emily,

Nels *is* in Paris! I have had one rather awkward meeting with him about which I shall tell you later when I am more certain of my feelings about it.

Hippolyte Dreyfus, you will be happy to learn, is progressing well with the translation into French of Laura's book. She has been collaborating with him on the translation. They have selected the title *Les Leçons de Saint Jean-d'Acre*. I should not be surprised, my dear, if they were soon to announce their engagement.

I'm off to a class, but wanted to dash this off before leaving.

———————

Paris
28 March 1910

Emily, my dear one,

I am somewhat more in control of myself now, though I am no closer to having sorted out the meaning of my meeting with Nels. It came about unexpectedly. Michael Athlone had invited Laura, Hippolyte and me to a poetry reading to hear John Allister, a young American quite unknown to me. Afterwards we stopped at a café for a small meal – remember the one on boulevard St Germain where we used to gorge ourselves on cream-filled pastries? Anyway, Nels came in with Amy Summerville, both looking a little flushed, and stopped briefly at our table. Nels' manner was supercilious; I felt that it was an attempt to cover his acute embarrassment. Michael was marvelous, displaying more warmth than usual in an effort to put Nels at ease; and Laura was, as always, magnificently gracious, remembering to congratulate Amy on the publication of her book and inviting them to join us. We were a strange sextette. Then Amy was whisked away by some of the young men who usually form part of her entourage, and the others gradually excused themselves by courteous design and left me with Nels who became instantly remorseful and apologetic, imploring forgiveness for having failed me – said he was sorry if he seemed to rebuff me but pride prevented his calling on me upon his return to Paris. On the way home, when we were quite alone on a deserted street, he began to weep. I found it unbearable and realized I had not seen a grown man weep before – it had never occurred to me that papa or Paul could weep. I was both touched and repelled. And when I comforted him he pulled back from my embrace with the words, 'Your eyes frighten me; I cannot be what you want me to be.' What sense can I make of this, Emily? How little I understand men!

I am greatly in awe of my father's austerity (though I know his heart is warm), and somewhat intimidated by Paul's assured and unquestioning grip on life which he manages with such authority balancing it like a ledger entry, all so tidily. And I am baffled by the conflicts which seethe in Nels, his potential greatness warring with – (with what? some unnamed fear or weakness?) And then there is Michael, whose secretiveness mystifies me. Do you know that he never speaks of his family? I have not told you that Michael and Hippolyte have been meeting frequently and have become fast friends. I have no doubt they discuss the Bahá'í Teachings in depth but Michael does not speak of it to me and I do not feel I should trespass by asking Hippolyte.

As I said, I am left to sift my feelings about Nels. Forgiving him for hurting me is the least part of that process. What right have I to admit hurt into my experience? That's the question I feel I should address to myself; but not until I draw closer to saintliness! I am a little horrified by the amount of pride and vanity I find residing like snug tenants in my bosom, yet my vacillating will, like an indifferent landlord, seems to lack the indignation that might inspire him to evict them.

———————

Paris
12 April 1910

My dear Mamma,

Praise, it seems, not only swells the head but has an adverse effect on the larynx. My performance in the student recital won from Prof Clémenceau an unusual degree of enthusiasm for my 'effortlessly spun phrases, firmly supported tone and lucid flexibility' – with the result that for the next few days I could not sing an unflawed note. And not even a head cold to blame it on. He has raised the question of whether I might spend some time in Rome before returning home or, failing that, in Stuttgart under the tutelage of his friend, Frau Gürtner, who was trained by Massenet. I should like to know what you and papa think of these suggestions. Of course, it would be premature to make a firm decision at this time, but it is perhaps to be considered for the future. When it is possible to make arrangements, Prof Clémenceau wants Massenet to hear me.

Emily writes that she will visit Boston to see her friend, Marie du Bédat, before leaving on her tour, and will call on you while she is there. I can hardly wait to see her again and, of course, if you and papa would reconsider and allow me to accompany Emily to the Holy Land, I would be very happy. Forgive me if I seem to press the question, but it is of great importance to me. I shall, of course, abide by your decision, for I would not wish to flout your wishes or cause you grief.

Thank you for inquiring about Mrs Maxwell. The harsh climate of Quebec is a great test for one of her uncertain health, but she is well and her letters are full of inspiration, reflecting perfectly her calm wisdom. May I share with you one jewel from her last letter? 'The mortal cage is nothing; the soul's motion in relation to the Beloved is the unfolding of all the meaning of life.' Isn't that a wonderful conception of existence? She is expecting her first child, a wish cherished since her marriage in 1902, so you can imagine her happiness and that of her many friends. Did I tell you? Her husband is a brilliant architect and a man of very noble qualities. What a blessed existence their child will have!

Ada has not written for weeks. Please let me know whether she is well. I have sent her a program from the concert.

You will note from the program that I sang Chausson's 'Les Heures' in the recital, and three Duparc songs, and a lovely setting Prof Clémenceau composed for the poem of a little-known French poet, Paul Valéry, '*Grand Soleil, qui sonnes l'éveil à l'être et de feux l'accompagnes, toi qui l'enfermes d'un sommeil trompeusement peint de campagnes* . . . ' an address to the Sun, that great shining orb 'which brings within the compass of vision the obscure presence of the soul.' The piece was enthusiastically received though I felt I did not do it justice. But he was very kind and embraced me after the recital – an unusual gesture for he is rather reserved. My gown was a pale blue slipper-satin. A friend, Sybil, Edith Sanderson's sister, loaned me for luck a pair of small sapphire earrings that she had worn in a recital of Massenet's work. Some of the friends sent me roses and held a small celebration – I felt every inch a diva! But when I returned to my room and took off my finery and brushed out my hair I felt strangely depressed and flat and alone. I stood before the mirror and decided I didn't like my appearance, that my voice is unsatisfactory, that I am wasting my time here. A wave of homesickness swept over me and I cried a little and felt ever so much better for it.

I do not think I really want success if the cost is the plunging to the depths of depression after soaring in heights of elation! Thus I addressed my pillow as I fell asleep. But when morning came everything seemed normal and I was more than usually hungry, and stepped into the street feeling like a very ordinary girl who has the extraordinary good fortune to be in beautiful, beautiful Paris. I almost began singing in the street, I felt so happy!

I am working on three exquisite songs by Fauré, one of which persistently eludes me. Fortunately his exalted duties as director of the Conservatory prevent his hearing my attempts to render it. 'Sing the song,' Prof Clémenceau admonishes, 'don't martyr it.'

———

Paris
26 May 1910

Emily, dear,

I wrote to you about the strained reunion with Nels and the stormy scenes which followed. We are more at ease now, thank heaven, but I know he is drinking too much and he seems to have adopted a cynical outlook that ill becomes him. He laughs to excess and makes caustic comments – on the whole, his attitude and demeanor are very false. I feel I might help him if I could only break through the artificial shell with which he surrounds himself.

Sometimes, and most uncharitably, I wonder whether he plays on my sympathy without being aware of it, as a means of binding me to him, and therefore resists my efforts to communicate with him except on the most superficial level. But then I remind myself that he has been deeply hurt and that it is my duty, as a Bahá'í, to warm the chilled heart and be a balm to the suffering. No, I err in saying 'duty'. To do the correct and natural and loving thing is merely to be fully human, a privilege rather than a duty. It is interesting how our old attitudes and vocabulary follow us into the Cause of Bahá'u'lláh and how all need re-defining in the light of His revelation.

Nels is writing no poetry at all, or says he isn't, and he sneers at the efforts of the Athlone group. 'Backward-looking and bathetic,' he says of them. 'They're forever tripping over their over-blown adjectives and laundering their lavender sins in public.' I see a little of Amy Summerville's influence in his new mannerisms of speech. Please pray for him, Emily, and pray for me too, that if I cannot awaken faith and hope in him that at least I do not stand in the way of his finding them. Perhaps the time has passed when I can be a channel, yet so far he does not respond to any of the other believers, although he respects Laura and Hippolyte. Where does responsibility to another soul begin and end? Are we to abandon the unresponsive heart and pass on to another more receptive listener?

Ah well, next month you will be here, and that will be good for me. I count the days. Do you know that I have days when I cannot pray, and faith seems as remote as the Himalayan mountains!

Dear Paul,

I am very grateful that you wrote explaining Ada's silence – I had begun to fear that I had hurt her in some way, and mamma's vague reference to 'Ada not being herself' far from having the effect mamma hoped for caused me considerable alarm. A certain degree of despondency is quite natural after the loss of the baby, but what you have told me suggests that Ada is far from normal in withdrawing into grief to the extent you describe. She is so deeply sensitive! Surely now, more than ever, she will need your understanding and comforting support. If there is anything I can do to help, please let me know at once.

I am sorry that you feel the prayer I sent to Ada served only to focus her attention on morbid thoughts and I quite understand your asking me not to aggravate her mental state by referring to such matters again. How far that result was from my intention! She wrote to me saying she found considerable comfort in prayer. Perhaps, Paul, if you could gently encourage her to talk about her feelings, she would not feel so isolated. Forgive me for presuming to offer advice, but I love you both very much, and love and concern incline one to take (perhaps unwelcome) liberties. I hope you will keep me advised about Ada's progress, and I assure you that I will respect your wishes. I hope the children have not noticed anything amiss. Tell them that I think of them very often and miss them very much. They will be quite grown up when I return.

I have been formally introduced to the songs of one Herr Franz Peter Schubert – a rest from my French adventures – but that esteemed gentleman may not, from his heavenly perch, appreciate the honor.

Paul, could you recommend some books to me? I always take delight in meeting new authors. But please do not direct me to any writers who are too relentlessly intent upon improving my mind nor any who are too dour. I have sampled Arnold Bennett's 'Clayhanger' and find his tone too ponderous. I had much enjoyed his 'The Old Wives' Tale' and my disappointment in his new work was heightened by recollection of the earlier book.

Emily and I had a wonderful reunion and three good weeks before she set out on her tour, accompanied by some friends from California. I longed to be one of the party but papa, as you know, was adamant. Emily will return by way of Italy so I shall not see her on her journey home. After seeing her father in New York she plans to visit Boston again and would like to see you and Ada, if you feel that would be appropriate. She spoke so warmly of you both and of your kindness to her when she last visited you.

The embroidered cloth Ada sent with Emily is so beautiful I almost hesitate to use it, but I could not quite resist displaying Ada's exquisite needlework to my appreciative friends. I shall write to Ada, of course, to express my gratitude, but first wanted to reply to you and assure you of my constant loving thoughts.

My studies go well, but my voice can never quite equal the tones I hear in my imagination nor satisfy Prof Clémenceau's expectations. Still, one day you might be proud of me.

Paris
16 September 1910

Dearest May,

The announcement of the birth of your Mary brought the greatest happiness to your many spiritual children. I literally wept with joy as I offered a prayer of thanksgiving. How bright must be the destiny of this child of the New Age who will be raised in the warm circle of your love!

I am ashamed to say how orphaned I felt after Emily's departure for the Holy Land, and could only rise above my self-pity by concentrating on my happiness for her. She has promised to send me a copy of her pilgrim notes and if you would wish it I shall gladly send you the account, though no doubt Emily herself will offer one to you. For a few nights after she left I had troubling dreams, one of them recurring as dreams sometimes will. In it, I stood on a rocky barren shore along the edge of the sea. In the distance, across the water, I could see a radiance which I knew to be the Shrine of Bahá'u'lláh. I was filled with an irresistible longing to journey there but could find no way of crossing the water. I called in my dream, asking whether I might approach, but no answer was forthcoming, only the sad liquid sound of the lapping waves, and I awakened each time flooded with desolation and a sense of unutterable loss. On the third day I composed a little melody and put some words to it, words which express in some measure the longing experienced in my dream. I call it 'Pilgrim Song':

Swift would I be, Lord, swift; on dancing feet
Hastening would come, if called, nor brook
　　delay,
Gleefully come – though lone the perilous way
And stern and starless – still would my step be
　　fleet;
And singing would come and, with song, entreat
Angels to chart my path. Though Thou might
　　slay
Me, still would I come and rejoicing stay
Quick or faint or slain at Thy welcoming feet.
Gifts would I bring – choice, my gifts, and many –
Laden with gifts, and laughing, would I come;
Or pauperized come – hands cupped, bereft of any
But hoarded hot tears – to stand before Thee,
　　dumb.
Swift would I be, Lord, if Thou wouldst but call –
My aim, my hope, my home, my love, my all.

I sang it for Nels one evening, hoping it might bring us closer, but when I had finished he only looked away and said it was a charming tune flawed by syrupy words of adolescent morbidity. It is strange that he no longer has the power to hurt me, but whether this is because I am growing freer of concern for the opinion of others or because I pity him, I cannot say. Perhaps we humiliate others by our pity, but I cannot help feeling sorry for Nels. He is retreating further and further into cynicism; soon, I fear, he will be beyond reach. Other than journalism, he is not writing. His work has brought him some recognition but he seems indifferent to it and he refuses to take anything seriously – Nels, who was always so earnest about everything! He still 'takes up' one cause after another, always playing with his new momentary enthusiasm as with a bauble. The theories of the Viennese scientist, Dr Sigmund Freud, are his latest interest and he is full of praise for *Die Traumdeutung* – but he is without *real* enthusiasm. And he is desperately unhappy. Why is the human heart so blind when the Sun of Reality is shining so manifestly!

Mr Struven has been with us recently, having completed the tour which he and Mr Remey undertook. Mr Remey, I understand, would have accompanied him to Europe but was called back to America for the marriage of his sister. Mr Struven, however, visited a number of centers in Europe following his pilgrimage. I took a few notes of his remarks concerning those blessed moments spent in the presence of 'Abdu'l-Bahá and am enclosing a copy for you. Mr Struven says that the work is progressing very well in Stuttgart where Dr Fisher's meetings are well attended. Dear Miss Knobloch, too, is a tireless worker and with noteworthy zeal is drawing many souls to the Teachings. Alma's travels to Esslingen, Zuffenhausen, Leipzig and Gera are producing wonderful results.

Your letters are shared among the friends. Let

me join their greetings to mine. The arrival of Mary must round out the happiness you and Mr Maxwell have found in your lives together.

Paris
12 April 1911

Dear Emily,

I am sorry, of course, about the death of your father but I can appreciate that the release from his suffering must have been welcome. It was touching beyond words that he should have asked you to read prayers in his last hours and told you that he wanted to be accepted as a believer. His welcome and progress in the next world are assured, and this must bring you great consolation.

Despite my father's attacks and my mother's frail health I have never imagined life without them, so huge a space do they seem to occupy in my existence. Death has not yet robbed me of one as close as your father must have been to you.

All the friends here are, of course, eager for news, especially about the work of the Bahá'í Temple Unity Committee, so never hesitate to pass along any items that come your way. The *Bahá'í News* is eagerly welcomed, but our hearts hunger for any news of progress of the work. We last read that there are now sixteen Assemblies in the United States and wonder whether the number has grown since then. The addition of a Persian section in *Bahá'í News* is a fine idea.

And now, my dear young lady, what *is* this

news you are being so secretive about? It was most unkind of you to tantalize me with veiled references to 'a certain young man'. I shall expect a full report as soon as decently possible! I should say a full, frank and comprehensive report, for if you are seriously interested in this brash fellow I must know *all*. I simply cannot have you marrying just *anyone*.

Your friendship with Juliet Thompson pleases me so much – already I love her from the stories the friends here have told me about her days in Paris; and the fact that she, too, is our beloved May's spiritual daughter makes her a sister, so of course she holds a warm place in my heart and I hope to meet her one day. I was most interested in your comments about her Lebanese friend, Kahlil Gibran, and look forward to reading his poetry. Have you seen any of his paintings? From all you say, the Kinney family must be wonderful. One day I shall have a chance to meet all your new friends.

Nels has left for Vienna to write a series of articles about Dr Freud's Psycho-Analytical Society, as well as some travel pieces. I am glad to say that Nels seems somewhat more assured these days, more like his former self. We are able to talk sometimes but I have felt it best to keep the conversation running along neutral lines, so I do not mention the Teachings in a direct way. He has tried once or twice to speak about marriage, but I think it is unwise to go into that painful subject – strange to use the adjective 'painful'! but you understand – at least right now. I wonder whether the attraction he feels for me is really an attraction towards whatever measure I reflect of the Teachings? Until I am more certain of this and how I should regard it, it seems best to assure him of my friendship and continue to pray for his healing. (Don't be mean and say that I should also pray for his protection!) Why can't guidance through prayer come written out in large clear letters on a sheet of paper and be delivered by celestial carrier pigeon? (Perhaps it does sometimes – I grow increasingly awed by divine confirmations!) But, I mean, *usually* it involves the creative and dangerous act of attempting to apply a divine principle, and the purifying of one's motives, and all those 'iffy' things. I know we can turn to the Master and ask for His advice but when I hear the pilgrims speak of His fatigue and the mountain of mail that descends upon Him from every quarter, I realize that we cannot forever behave like children, that we must grow up and learn to apply the divine pattern for living that His Father's Teachings gives us. Surely that is why we have them! But even recognizing *that*, why is it all so difficult?

For instance: what to do about, not only Nels, but my future studies in Rome or Stuttgart? Prof Clémenceau continues to encourage me to consider further study abroad, but I cannot press my parents too far. And I don't really know whether my motive in desiring further study is the progress of my singing or – yes, you have guessed it! – the idea that I might advance the work of the Cause, especially in Rome. Think of it – to establish a center in the very heart of Catholicism! Well, I am praying about all this, too, as you can imagine, but would like to know that my prayers were being reinforced by yours.

A curious encounter yesterday with Michael Athlone at the Stoughtons' dinner party. I am well aware of the breach in his relationship with Nels and was mildly surprised that in private conversation after dinner he should have inquired most ardently about him; I saw that he was fully aware of Nels' problems and filled with compassion and sympathy. Michael feels that Nels has remarkable gifts but that he could become merely a fluent and accomplished trifler, as he put it, a dilettante; or one of those, one might say, professional eccentrics who hang about the cafés airing their grievances and displaying their repertoire of mannerisms. I listened carefully for tones of malice in Michael's voice, but heard none, and realized that although Nels apparently has rejected him, Michael feels no ill will. In fact he expressed the hope that I could help Nels find himself and said he wanted to see me again to talk about 'my philosophy'. Of course he made the protest people often do about not wanting to be converted, and he claimed to be merely intellectually curious, but I wonder whether he is not perhaps a genuine seeker. I know he has had several talks with Hippolyte and that their friendship is deeply based. I have rarely seen such warm compassion as he displayed when asking about Nels. I'm having dinner with him next week, and I've asked Laura to arrange an evening with some of the friends, including Hippolyte. On an impulse, I've invited Amy Summerville, too.

I do not get to the galleries very often without

you here to goad and educate me, but Michael has offered to take me to see the work of Gustav Klimt whose portraits he has praised. 'You'll like their extravagance and vitality,' he persuaded. In my mind I heard the echo of your cautionary retort, 'We'll see.' However, I murmured something appropriate.

————————

Paris
3 June 1911

Dear Maggie,

I hasten to assure you that you are not out of turn in writing – I am delighted to know that Ada is very much her old self. Bless your heart for letting me know! As you may guess, I have been very worried and it is good to know that she is progressing to the extent that Sunday dinners with mamma and papa are the normal pattern again. Be assured that I will not refer to your letter when I write to mamma, and that I appreciate your concern. I've consulted the second Book of Samuel and shall 'Tell it not in Gath, publish it not in the streets of Askelon.'

Now, as for the other matter you mentioned, I scarcely know what to think – but I will do all I can, you may be sure. Although I am very touched that Paul should have defended to papa my request to join Emily on her visit to the Holy Land, I am saddened to think that I should have been the cause of a quarrel of such bitterness. Do you think I should write to Paul about it? His sympathy brings tears to my eyes and I must confess surprises me. You remember how it was when we were children – I never felt that Paul quite approved of me and I grew timid about drawing close to him – despite your gentle efforts to bring us together, to interpret me to him. I was always so fanciful, and he was – just dear, practical Paul. My conversations with him were so stilted; I hope Ada has not noticed this same quality in my letters. I truly love them both.

It was always fruitless to try to conceal anything from you. Your gift for patching things up between people will no doubt assure you of a throne in heaven. Remember how you reconciled Mrs McAllister and her cook after they had that silly misunderstanding about the tradesmen's accounts? Kate spread it through the neighborhood that you were a defender of the oppressed, but I am sure your fame has reached the ears of angels.

Speaking of cooks, I was recently served a dish that made me think of you – roast chicken with prune and green pepper and coconut dressing. 'It would never occur to Maggie to stuff a chicken with those ingredients,' I thought to myself, wishing heartily that it had never occurred to my hostess. I did not trouble to ask her for the recipe for your collection!

Emily, my dear,

I have been hoping for the opportunity to write to you for days, and now a mild throat infection which has confined me to my rooms provides the chance for my doing so without interruption. A strange letter came from Maggie last week – written in strict confidence and filled with profuse apologies for speaking out of turn, etc., – and informing me that Ada has regained her good spirits and is pregnant again. *But*, papa and Paul have quarreled bitterly over papa's refusing to allow me to accompany you to the Holy Land. Whatever you said on your last visit apparently captured Paul's interest and sympathy, and he expressed the view at dinner with the family that papa was too strict and interfering – words to that effect. Perhaps not really fair to papa who, after all, has sanctioned my being in Paris without a chaperone and with only the kindly Stoughtons, who are only distantly related, to keep an eye on me. However, a violent scene ensued during which Paul argued that I should be given opportunity for travel while I am on the Continent, tactlessly pointing out that my legacy from grandmother Edison, which as you know he manages for me, provides me with the financial independence for travel and further study, and warning that father's authoritarian attitude could result in my throwing myself into an unsuitable marriage to achieve my freedom, and so on. All very ugly, and none of it escaping Maggie's sharp ear for drama or her revulsion for anything that threatens to weaken family relationships. Separated as she is from her own relatives who are few in number and scattered to the four winds, she is fierce in her efforts to preserve unity; and, of course, we are, in a sense, an extension of her family by links of loyalty, affection and long service though not by ties of blood.

Maggie asks that I do what I can to heal the rupture, although I must say I can think of little to do from this distance, especially since I am not supposed to know about it. Perhaps an opening will occur as a result of mamma's next letter, or Paul's, if he writes again. Meanwhile, I can only try to say nothing to aggravate the situation. Both papa and Paul are strong-willed and inclined to what I suppose could be called pride in their wrong-headedness, and forgiveness comes slowly to their natures.

I am very happy for Ada – because of her pregnancy, I mean – and delighted about her having regained her normal balance, but still she does not write to me and I worry in case I have ineptly turned her against the Teachings. In one part of my mind I realize that it is very human to turn one's thoughts to the Creator in time of difficulty and to neglect Him when life is smooth, but there may be a less apparent explanation. All of which causes me to wonder what becomes of those who enter the orbit of the Cause and feel an attraction, but make another choice? We cannot judge, of course, but the matter causes me to wonder. I suppose our course is to pray that they realize the door is always open and not to bar their way by our condemnation. We who have been privileged to accept the gift of faith must confirm our acceptance in every breath, at every moment of our lives, recognizing that even after a lifetime of devoted service we can, in our last breath, cast the gift aside – I think of this when I read Bahá'u'lláh's words to the effect that all in heaven and earth cling to His garment. Do not think I pity or condescend to Ada. I bear the name 'believer in His Cause' but I am far from exemplifying the Bahá'í attributes that characterize her life. I might be barred from heaven's gate forever by sheer envy of her seeming innate goodness. We are all alone in treading the path to Him – how grateful I am to have your friendship on this journey!

Michael has been pressing me to tell him what the Cause *really* is and has been very patient (sometimes I think even receptive!) about my attempts to express my understanding of it. We have had a series of talks and I have learned that he sees some of the other friends, in addition to Hippolyte, and asks them the same questions. He reads whatever he is given to read and obviously thinks about it, and then returns with more questions. I think we have captured his curiosity, his mind, as it were, and it remains to see whether his heart will be touched. He is well known here through his work at the publishing house and has access to the literati; he could be an outstanding worker in the Cause. I am grateful that he understood when I said that in my opinion the Bahá'ís grasp but dimly what the Cause really is or what will be the effects in future of our feeble efforts to serve the Divine Will. I do not think we can know yet what we are building that is implied in the words 'the Kingdom of God on earth.' We surely have no more idea than the earliest Christians did of what they were doing. How could those simple souls have foreseen the great Cathedrals – not that they are Christianity but they are symbols of the Christian aspiration and triumph – or how could they have imagined that the Hand of God would work through history to elevate the Cause of Christ? I often think that a measure of the validity of Christ's Teachings is that the lives of people like my parents, these long centuries later, should be informed by Christ's words. The only real difference is that my family have not yet recognized that the Sun of His truth has now dawned on another point of the horizon and illuminates those matters He referred to when He said that He had many things to tell us but we could not bear them at an earlier time. Reflecting on this fills me with a deep love for my parents and strengthens my determination to acquire the patience the Master bids me to.

Michael, I should add, was right. I was thrilled by Klimt's paintings. There is something lush and tangled and almost dangerous just beneath their surfaces, but his vision is strictly controlled by a steely discipline which prevents their erupting before your very eyes into confusion. They are very warm and his models stare out at you like nuncios who might whisper messages of vast import. I liked best his 'Expectations' – a beautiful woman clasping her head and presenting to the viewer her expressionless face as though to ask 'Is this what you expect of me?' And you know that she will present any face or be any aspect of 'woman' the viewer demands of her.

Michael has told me that he is very impressed by Hippolyte's book and his essays and he commented that the Bahá'ís will have increasing need of scholars. He is drawn, of course, to what I might call the poetry of our Writings, but does not fully trust that level of response.

But, dearest, this letter is growing far too long (and is small compensation for my not having you here to talk to) and I have as yet said nothing about your Peter! And what is there for me to say except that I am very happy for you? The fact that he has fallen in love with you already places him at the center of my affections, and his acceptance of the Cause doubles my joy. Will you announce your engagement soon? You must let me know as soon as you have made your plans so that I may savor every moment. I have placed the photograph you sent in my prayerbook and look at it often. Yes, yes, I agree – Peter has *wonderful* eyes! And you look – oh, radiant and vulnerable and sweet. Even more luminous than I remember. I would not have guessed that Peter is a lawyer, though you had mentioned that before; my first thought would have been a musician – those marvelous hands! There is a light tenderness in his face that blends with the intelligence to devastating effect. I am surely not wrong in thinking that you were the object of that tenderness at the moment the photograph was taken. Have you attempted Peter's portrait? You know, my dear, that I wish you every happiness. Are you not just a little frightened? As long as love is a destination toward

which you travel you can feed on expectation –
but to have arrived at the destination; does it not
somewhat overwhelm you with its finality and
unforeseen demands? I wish I could understand or
experience that certainty you speak of. I cannot
quite imagine how it feels to have love step
forward and seize your hand and point to a face
among the crowd and say 'Yours to cherish
forever' and have your doubt and scepticism drain
away. I see it as a flood of peace, as when death
might appear – but it frightens me. Perhaps one
day I'll know.

———————

Paris
1 July 1911

Dear Mamma,

I was most disturbed to hear that papa has had
another attack, caused by a misunderstanding
with Paul, and I know what anguish this must
cause you. This sad circumstance will surely
underline the importance of papa avoiding
situations that cause stress. Poor Paul! How
dreadful he must feel! I truly appreciate your
frankness in telling me of this, for although I can
do little but pray, I should not want to be
uninformed of the matters that press in upon
those I love.

It was very dear of papa to suggest that I might
consider breaking my studies for a few weeks and
devote them to seeing something of Europe, and I
shall certainly avail myself of this opportunity,

but first I would wish to be assured that papa is making progress in his convalescence or I should not be able to enjoy myself. Please, mamma, keep me closely informed, and thank papa for his generosity. I, too, feel that I would benefit from a rest, and our summers here are all too brief.

I was the guest of Laura Clifford Barney at *Don Giovanni* last week, a superb production with Lilli Lehmann and Edouard de Reszke. I have observed that there is nothing like exposure to perfection to reduce my aspirations to size.

Paris
6 July 1911

Dear Emily,

Do you recognize the author of this?

Rebirth

My scattered atoms prayed, 'Love, make us
    whole,'
As clay implores the craftsman mould the pot.
Gently did Love knead and smooth and roll
The delicate and lovely thing he wrought.
With tender gaze he raised a mighty hand
And ground the fragile artefact to sand.
I begged that he design the form anew
To his own plan, a stouter vessel fashion;
Fiercely was it pummeled, shaped more true,
And fused to strength within the kiln of passion.
These sterner curves the flames but lately kissed
Love, smiling, dashed once more with smiting
    fist.

Clay pleads, till cast as Potter might ordain,
Come Kneader, shape and shatter me again.

I found a handwritten draft of this sonnet between the pages of a book I borrowed from Michael, and was excited at the thought that it might be his, which he admitted. When I asked if I might keep it he seemed embarrassed and said it was worthless, a school-boy's exercise.

'But I like it,' I said.

'Can't you see that it's derivative?' he protested in mild anger. 'Any fool can string words together; the point is to have experienced them.'

'The poem speaks to me, do let me have it,' I urged. 'Surely in writing it you expressed something that you truly felt.'

'Only the idea was experienced; it was the working out of an idea. We write about those things that cause us unrest,' Michael said.

But he let me keep it. The clay is restless, Emily!

———————

Paris
10 July 1911

Dear Paul,

You must not blame yourself so harshly. Perhaps you are right in thinking that you struck out at papa's rigidity because it is a quality you recognize and detest in yourself; who can say? I know all too well that self-recognition is painful. What is important, however, is that you forgive yourself and make every effort to become reconciled to papa, for although he does not readily display emotion he is very distressed and, of course, mamma is beside herself.

You have certainly succeeded in making a point with papa, for he has suggested that I take a rest from my studies for a few weeks and spend some time traveling; it would be helpful if you would reinforce my efforts to let him know this is appreciated. In his own awkward way, he loves us both, and this is his means of admitting that your remarks hit their mark. And do not think I am unappreciative of your efforts to obtain more freedom for me, dear Paul.

Travel! I am tempted to see Italy, of course, but I feel the time is not right. Nels has recommended Austria – he was there recently to write some articles and has returned full of enthusiasm for it – but I am drawn to the Alps and to England. I must confess it is not just the majestic scenery of the mountains or the wonders of London that draw me, but – you will laugh at me! – a dream I had which I will not horrify you by relating. I know you would not hesitate to remind me what a state of bedlam the world would be in if everyone, including statesmen and bankers and school marms, based their decisions on the vagaries of dreams.

I am so pleased that you were able to see Emily and her fiancé, Peter Alderton, during their recent visit to Boston. Though I've not met Peter I, too, feel it is a good match.

Emily, dear –

Having just completed a letter to Paul I write in haste for I wish this to catch the afternoon post. Your visit to Paul has caused him to do a considerable amount of soul searching (incidentally, he fully approves of Peter and thinks you are well suited!) and the brunt of his letter was an exploration of those aspects of his nature which he sees reflected in papa – or which he thinks he has inherited from father – and to which he reacted so negatively. Now he feels he must direct attention to correcting his own shortcomings. It was quite the warmest, frankest letter he has written to me, full of self-doubts and misgivings – very touching. And I think he has solved the mystery of Ada's recent aloofness. I told you, I think, that her letters have been infrequent and almost formal of late. Paul says she recognized before he did that he was becoming sympathetic to my interest in the Cause and she began to resent it. In her depressed condition, she interpreted Paul's sympathy for me as a form of withdrawal from her which seemed especially cruel when she needed his full attention. She reacted by dropping her interest in the Teachings and growing more depressed. Finding herself pregnant again, Ada resolved to go through the motions of living a normal life but matters came to a head when Paul and papa had their altercation, and now Ada and Paul have brought their feelings into the open for the first time and have been drawn closer together. Paul feels their marriage has been strengthened by the experience and says that perhaps later they will investigate the Cause together; but first, he feels, they must continue to improve their relationship. Your visit helped a great deal and Paul spoke – uncharacteristically again – of your 'infectiously happy and balanced view of life.' You can imagine how grateful I am to you, dear.

Paul said that he came upon you playing with the children and then later saw the obvious delight they took in sitting for the sketches you made, and hearing their laughter he felt suddenly a total stranger to Bethany and Roland who seemed so at ease with you. It strikes me that this was the key for him. Perhaps to a degree I have never suspected he suffers from a sense of remoteness from papa and wants to be close to his own children. Strange that it is rarely our conscious efforts that affect another – what we choose to say or do in order to influence them – but the spontaneous phrase or gesture. God achieves through our innocence what we cannot through our calculation.

I must fly now. Dinner with Michael and Nels! With considerable effort and good will on both sides, perhaps aided by ardent prayers on my part, they have agreed to resume their friendship. Tonight's dinner is therefore in the nature of a celebration. I would be content to leave it at that, but there is the added possibility that Nels will succeed in interesting Michael in publishing a novel he has been working on secretly, and so the evening will probably be in the nature of a business meeting. (Men! she exclaimed, stamping her foot and tossing her auburn curls!) However, I plan not to let their discussion lessen my appetite. And I am bursting to know what Nels' novel is about.

Nels is open and talkative again, almost like old times. He seems not the least jealous of the time I have been spending with Michael. *Not* very flattering, is it? Michael has mentioned that to me, in fact, in one of his candid moments. Later I realized he was really suggesting that Nels' efforts at renewing the friendship with him are at least in part inspired by a need to ingratiate himself with me. When we next met, I accused Michael of harboring unfounded suspicions and of being altogether too analytical.

'Well,' he replied, 'analysis is the disease of this century,' and with a weary sigh turned to other topics. Anyway, I shall allow none of these tortuous considerations to spoil what is certain to be a sumptuous dinner at which I shall be seated between two handsome escorts. My blue worsted skirt fits me again, a sure indication that my exercising has had beneficial results, at least for my waist, so I feel entitled to one rather generous meal.

I thrilled to see Nijinsky in Fokine's new ballet 'The Specter of the Rose'. Ah, Nijinsky – now there's a subject worth a portrait – part god, part ghost. There is something haunted about him, something doomed and terrible, as though he sees that the perfume of his own beauty will turn upon and destroy him.

———

Dear Emily,

I am delighted to have news of your commission for the portrait of Commander Arnold and consider it to your credit, both artistic and spiritual, that you resisted the temptation to move his hairline forward two inches and increase the girth of his chest. I'm sure it is such devious practices that have given artists a bad name among the general citizenry. Of course, when I sit for my portrait as *prima donna* I shall not object to your trimming my waist by a discreet inch or two, or adjusting any of my features to conform to a more ideal standard. I still have and greatly cherish the rapid sketch you did of me sitting at Laura's piano when I accompanied Edith Sanderson's sister, Sybil.

Michael and Nels have at last made peace but it was hard won. Michael did not like Nels' book and urged him to make changes; Nels was adamant. The senior editors saw the likelihood of the book's having good sales and have agreed to proceed with publication. Michael felt, apparently, that Nels wrote below the standard of his gift in the pose of 'enfant terrible', that the book lacks commitment and intensity, and was written with a view to dazzling the populace. He argued that the idea, the core, of the book was brilliant, but the writing was flashy and clever and facile. Rows ensued and some compromise was reached which satisfied the senior editors, and so it will proceed.

Michael, you may guess, does not like to com-promise; for that very reason he refuses to publish his own work, the juvenilia, and will wait until he feels he has a sufficient body of mature poems to offer. However, the firm having accepted Nels' book, Michael has committed himself to lend every assistance to ensure its success. He has an admirable integrity.

Curiously, he confided – well, it slipped out inadvertently, really, when we were alone – that at one point in their heated discussions he realized that he and Nels were, in disagreeing about the book, disagreeing on a deeper level and that I was the symbol at the center of the controversy. 'We see you differently,' Michael said; then, regarding Nels, he remarked, 'If an artist does not respect his own gift, can he truly respect someone he professes to love?' A great deal followed, not all of it pleasant for me. I remember with particular chagrin Michael exclaiming, 'Don't make of Nels your personal dancing bear. If you don't love him, let the man go. There are others who will gladly seize his chain if he needs to be someone's performing pet.'

When the hurt protest that was forming on my lips was overcome and I was in control of myself, I recognized that only one who cared for me would have made such a remark. I said, simply, 'Thank you,' and Michael flushed and apologized for speaking out of turn and scurried away as quickly as he could, but not before I told him that I was grateful for his kindness. Michael is a true friend. He never fails to give me food for thought when he breaks his customary silence and drops that mantle of courtesy in which he cloaks himself.

The wedding of Laura and Hippolyte was a wonderful event, quiet and dignified and elegant. Laura was more striking than ever, her aristocratic face lighted from within and heightening her beauty. You know how regally she carries herself and how tastefully she dresses. Imagine her, then, in an eggshell crêpe de Chine suit with a small corsage of coral rosebuds, a beaming Hippolyte beside her, looking as though he'd won life's first prize.

I overheard one guest say of them (as will be said of you and Peter!) 'A brilliant match,' and wondered whether she guessed the inner brilliancy of the union, of which their outer bearing is but a token. Their appearance distinguishes them wherever they go and they continue to be tireless in their service. They are very happy.

The friends here are astir in expectation of 'Abdu'l-Bahá's visit, and the physical preparations are but a modest reflection of the internal ones all are making. I am both elated and terrified. I begged Laura to tell me what to expect and what is expected of me but she merely laughed and said that there are no conventions applicable to visits to the environs of heaven. 'But you've been in His presence so often, surely you can help me prepare an adequate response,' I cried.

'Does one respond to each new sunrise in the same way?' she asked.

Oh Emily, why do we feel more secure with protocols? Why do we demand formulae?

Paris
24 August 1911

MISS EMILY PRIOR
STE. 243 SUTCLIFFE MANOR
143 RIVERSIDE DRIVE N.Y.N.Y.
JULIET ARRIVED SAFELY PARIS ENROUTE THONON
LES BAINS STOP TOMORROW WE ATTAIN PRESENCE
MASTER STOP DELIRIOUS WITH JOY STOP ALLAH-
UABHA. LOVE ALTHEA.

Hotel du Parc
Thonon-les-Bains
28 August 1911

Dear Emily,

Did my cablegram make sense? I cannot claim
to be responsible for anything I have said or done
or written since Hippolyte announced the
expected arrival of 'Abdu'l-Bahá; but despite the
intense excitement that has gripped us all since
that news reached Paris, we have somehow
contrived to do whatever was necessary to bring
us into the presence of the Master. Your Juliet
arrived and I loved her on sight. We have made
our way here – I had almost written to Paradise –
and are a party of perhaps eighteen or twenty in
number; difficult to know, for our ranks swell
with new friends arriving daily. Mr and Mrs
Horace Holley, two American friends, sped here
from Siena two days ago – and so it has gone. Oh,
if you and May were here to share this!

I had never dreamed that my pilgrimage would

occur at the Hotel du Parc, but here among sweeping manicured lawns and banks of luxuriant rhododendron I have come face to face with the Servant of the Supreme. How different this is from the grim and inhospitable setting of 'Akká which I have heard described so often by pilgrims, or the gentler but still austere quarters in which you met Him in Haifa before His departure for Egypt.

The futility of words! Now I understand in some small measure the indefinable bond of silent worshipful kinship that links those who have met the Master – for who, having glimpsed the ideal of human grace and perfection made manifest, can force that vision into the inadequate container of language? When I am not embracing the weeping Juliet and bidding her to dry her tears, I am myself struggling unsuccessfully against an inordinate desire to weep, for there seems no more natural response to that holy presence, and I find myself in Juliet's arms as she bids me, with misted eyes and a breaking, hoarse whisper, to control myself. We are a soggy duet!

Having yourself been in His presence you would have laughed heartily if you could have seen the care with which I chose my wardrobe for this journey – and now I scarcely know what I wear. This is one way of saying I see myself abandoning one world for another. I had not imagined it would be this way. I came laden with notebooks and questions, rehearsed requests and responses. I blush with shame remembering the artful curtsy I thought I might adopt when meeting Him – I tried it out before my mirror to see whether I could look both pretty and reverent. I had even thought, if the opportunity presented itself, to pursue points that I knew would interest Michael when I reported them to him, and composed in my mind a plea for personal guidance in dealing with Nels and the attitude of my family.

But all this fled away in that first moment of meeting 'Abdu'l-Bahá. I realized that the plane of words and appearances is not the one on which one truly and most productively meets Him. He moves far above the plane of rational thought and personality and raw emotion – although one may approach Him there. But it is on a divine level, in the sphere of the soul, that He is found. Here one sees – what shall I say? – the world as a mirage, an ash heap, and oneself as a caged bird with the potential to soar in the greatest joy and freedom to nest in the bosom of God in unalterable happiness.

His every word, glance and gesture call forth one's reality; the sinister barriers of self-interest, intellect, acquired knowledge, egotism, empty social conventions; the considerations of class and stature and prestige – all that might hold one back from His world – become unendurable, and one knows with certainty they *can* be overcome. And one understands – in a great calm the understanding dawns – that no effort can be too great if it will result in one's moving upward to live on the plane of consciousness where He dwells, patiently smiling, constantly beckoning: Upward, children, upward!

As Juliet and I sat gazing at Lake Leman in the last few moments of twilight as the earliest stars began to dot the deep mauve sky, music and voices drifted down from the terraces of the great hotel which rose in a dim white outline behind us. With its muted winking lights the building might have been the skyline of a doomed city we had fled for the closer and more intimate reality of the lake shore. It was as though we were the only people alive in that moment. I told Juliet I could die at that instant without regret.

'But you must live,' she admonished, 'to serve the Master!'

'But do we not pray to render a service in both worlds?' I asked.

'Be that as it may,' said Juliet, 'we are in this world to serve.'

And I agreed, for I saw, even in that vanishing light, her eyes brimming with tears and I did not wish to say more. But truly, Emily, I knew then and I know now, I would be well content to leave this world. In the same breath I confess that I have never loved the world more, nor felt more a part of it, for it is the mirror image of a higher reality and reflects great truth and beauty.

I have in these past few days achieved what for lack of better words I must call a heightened perspective — it is as though the Master had removed obscuring veils from my eyes and I see for the first time all things illuminated by the radiance of His world. All the ties of loyalty and friendship, and the subtle, steely filaments of emotion which bind me to those I love, including my family and Nels – and Michael, even – I see more clearly and dispassionately in this clearer, stronger light. I see them all as aspiring souls and feel an almost impersonal and pure sympathy for them, a love greater than I ever felt, by virtue of its detachment. I have lost all fear of Paul, of Amy Summerville – anyone who has ever intimidated me – all might be swept up in my exuberant embrace.

Even the aged porter I momentarily encountered today who has a rather venal face and an unattractive, obsequious manner, is bathed in this wash of sympathy. I took pains to express appreciation for some small and quite ordinary service he rendered. Something of my sincerity and intensity must have communicated itself – he looked quite startled, and dropping his servile mask he spoke to me in his *own* voice; we met as two souls, as it were. It lasted but a moment, but I counted it a victory for both of us; we dealt with each other on the plane of reality. Perhaps this is what being a Bahá'í is about; certainly it is the Master's way. The experience left me feeling wonderfully elated. Oh, to be able to see everyone as through the Master's eyes! How different our lives would be.

I think sleep will be impossible for me tonight, but I must close my eyes for a while at least. Juliet is writing in her diary but her eyes, too, are drooping. We are both wrung out, as you can imagine. I shall continue this tomorrow in a quiet moment.

I have taken no notes of the Master's words! My notebook sits untouched on the table looking rather sheepish and superfluous. But this is not an experience that can be reduced to notes – at least I do not find it possible now – and for the first time I understand why the pilgrims apologize for the skimpy accounts they produce of their moments with the Master and seek to emphasize the answers they have recorded to the questions they put to Him. Of course! The time spent in His presence is *personal*, an incommunicable interlude; but His words are for the world. Words serve admirably to convey information, but in addition to information He gives us Light, Example, Vision and so much more.

His reunion with the friends who have attained His presence in the Holy Land was touching beyond measure. When He said aloud in English 'Juliet Thompson' I could have died with pleasure.

Goodnight, my dear. I send you kisses in my thoughts; may they alight gently on your pillow to greet your soul when it awakens in the morning. Oh Emily, I have never felt closer to you than I do in this moment, through our love for Him! Now I see the source of May's incredible gift for loving all who cross her path – she loves them *through* Him and thus she is a celestial magnet. Again, goodnight.

———

Hotel du Parc
28 August 1911

Dear Nels,

You should be here. This is too great to miss. I shall try to carry it all home to you.

Hotel du Parc
28 August 1911

Dear Michael,

You would like Horace Holley, an American poet who has had work accepted by 'New Republic', 'Forum', 'Poetry' and other journals. He is gathering his poems for publication in New York by Mitchell Kennerley. Let me copy out for you a segment of 'Divinations':

Not in your eyes that look to hill and cloud,
Nor in your hand plucking the yellow blossom
Does Spring return,
But in My radiant will
That burns upon the winter of your heart!
In this Season,
Wherever the seeds of your endeavor strike,
There is renewal.

Oh Michael, if you could be here to meet 'Abdu'l-Bahá, to enter a presence that renews hope for the perfectibility of humankind!

Hippolyte and Laura join me in sending warmest greetings.

———

Hotel du Parc
29 August 1911

Dear Emily,

It will not surprise you if I say that Juliet and I talked far into the night, lingering at one of the small candlelit tables on the terrace in spite of the evening's chill, too unsettled to go to our rooms. I was curious to know why Juliet wept as she put down her diary and I gently asked her about it, fearing I might be intruding on some reflection too personal to share. Without a word she passed her journal to me, and I read:

If He never gave me so much as a word,
If He never glanced my way,
Just to see that sweetness shining before me
I would follow Him on my knees,
Crawling behind Him in the dust forever.

Juliet's consuming love for the Master will be her armor, her anchor, her epitaph. She let me copy her words and I offered to compose a melody for them so that she might have a private song to express her adoration which seems to wax greater each day. Thinking of this, I said, 'But you have been in His presence before, when you were in 'Akká in 1909. Can one never exhaust the joy and knowledge to be garnered from the privilege of being with Him?' In voicing the question I had a terrible moment in which I saw myself, in rapid succession, as deluded by His powerful charm, and then grown impervious to it – saw myself trying helplessly to raise defences against the scorn of Nels and the polite indifference of my family and the Episcopalian friends of my childhood – all of this in a split second.

Juliet's answer came with a rushing force. 'Each time I see Him it is different. Light shifts from hour to hour across a landscape revealing new details, illuminating in one moment a tree, in another a cloud and in yet another a pebble or field flower. As light is inexhaustible, so is the presence of 'Abdu'l-Bahá. Surely you have seen this: He is at one instant a King, at another a Teacher or loving Father, and then again the gracious host or the humblest of servants. But whether He is seen as the embodiment of humility or majesty, it is for the soul's training. At first, I saw only a blinding radiance which overwhelmed me, causing me, I think, to be oblivious to everything else about Him. Then, for a time, I think I adored the personality, the attributes. But we grow in understanding. I think now the Glory of God, the Eternal Face of Bahá'u'lláh, has revealed itself to me in Him. 'Abdu'l-Bahá has unveiled His face and it is – on the human plane – a reflection of the Face of Bahá'u'lláh. Everywhere, now, I see that face – its majesty, its effulgence, its immortal beauty.'

We grew still and sat listening to the sound of crickets rising faintly in the distance as though Nature were providing a chorus of affirmation to Juliet's words – *Yes! Yes!* – when we were joined briefly by Mr Holley who also was reluctant or unable to sleep. He is a spare man with the controlled manner and intense face of an intellectual. I wondered what might the Master have meant to him, one so unlike myself and Juliet; but when our eyes met I knew there was no need to speak of it for I saw a personal reverence of a degree unfortunately rare in a Western man. When we spoke it was of the words we had heard the Master utter earlier in the day, that even in the West martyrs would be found for the Cause. We used the word 'martyr' awkwardly – it was strange on the tongue – and I found myself thinking of my Bahá'í friends and who among them might be called to this station. May's lovely face suddenly loomed before me and I shrank from the image with a shiver, almost expressing aloud the small cry which rose in my throat.

Juliet said that the journey of 'Abdu'l-Bahá to the West was unprecedented in religious history and might well be among the most significant events to be associated with His ministry. 'But He has suffered so severely,' she added, 'and He is now in His sixty-eighth year – and in broken health – how will the callous West receive him?'

'Surely as He has been received here,' I exclaimed, remembering the reverent hush that fell across the rooms of the hotel as He swept through that cosmopolitan gathering followed by His Oriental entourage. On no face could be seen amusement or idle curiosity. Here and there someone spontaneously bowed his head or rose in respect as He passed.

Mr Holley nodded agreement. 'I shuddered to think of Him in the dehumanizing atmosphere of Western cities,' he said, 'but the thought occurred that there more than anywhere will He demonstrate, indeed embody, the essential contrast between spirit and matter. He will tower above the cities; He is greater than railroads, than sky scrapers, than banks and trusts and the other institutions of man.'

'That's it,' I said, 'for He stands at the Center of Spirit, the Center of Reality.'

And as I fell asleep later, my own words kept echoing in my head: He is at the Center of Reality, and the Essential Reality is God's Covenant with man. Might He not be the Center of that Covenant? But sleep engulfed me before I could carry the thought further. Only in the morning did I realize that I had forgotten to say my prayers! Thus are we protected from spiritual vanity!

Next day:

While I was dressing my hair this morning – and despite my indifference to the task and the haste with which I performed it – a little song formed in my mind:

> His days, His life a Scripture,
> Chapter and verse I scan;
> In this celestial script discern
> The One Whose child I am.

Chorus: My longing has drawn me to cool places
> High on the mountain where the white deer run;
> Here the heart's sweet Huntsman has ensnared me,
> Here gives clear crystal water and the Sun.

> His smile, His voice a music
> To lure the lost child home.
> Will not Enchanter lead one
> Who seeks to be His own?

I must go, dear. You will understand that I cannot bear the thought of missing one single moment of these treasured days.

———

Hotel du Parc
29 August 1911

Dear Nels,

I've met Horace Holley, an American poet who has published here and there. He has praised the Irish poet William Yeats and shown me his 'In the Seven Woods'. I shall look for it in London and bring it to you when I come.

Please convey my best wishes to Amy and to Michael.

––––––

Hotel du Parc
29 August 1911

Dearest May,

But for you I should not be here. But for you I should not have entered beneath His shelter and found this peace that takes up residence in the heart as though the heart existed for no other tenant. Without your love and patience I should have been ill prepared to suffer His love which is both wound and balm. The very atoms of my body have been recreated in but one smile from His lips, and I tremble lest I fail to become all He would have me be.

May, how shall I thank you? Your name is frequently on His dear lips – queens and empresses might die to be so privileged. Pray for me. I feel inadequate to the overflowing cup I am offered.

––––––

Hotel du Parc
1 September 1911

Dearest Mamma,

These have been utterly heavenly days enhanced by the incredibly beautiful scenery and the companionship of Emily's friend, Juliet Thompson, an accomplished painter. It is not my wish to deceive you so I must say that the essential purpose of the days here has been to pay homage to 'Abbás Effendi, and it is my intention to proceed to London to take advantage again of the opportunity of learning from this great Spiritual Educator Who has come to the West to spread His Father's Teaching of the oneness of humankind. Oh mamma! I think if you were to spend but one moment in His presence it would allay your doubt, and your heart, like mine, would yearn to win His good pleasure, for He embodies the reality of the Christian Faith – of all Faiths.

When I told Him I was the daughter of a minister He beamed broadly and told me that being the daughter of a servant of God, I must also become a servant. The work of Christ was that of the Comforter, He said, and indicated that I too must take up the work of comforting the children of God. As we passed a charming little church in the countryside He gazed at it with a tender yearning and said He longed to attend the Sunday service. His all-pervasive sympathy obliterates division and separateness. He teaches that the basis of true religion, divested of outward trappings and rituals and formulas, is one. If you knew my happiness you would rejoice for me.

119

His most frequent injunction is *Be happy!* His first question in any gathering is *Are you happy?* His own abundant happiness and undimmed joy is ever overflowing in the most irresistible humor that completely captivates the heart and puts the lie to fear as an aspect of the spiritual life. He smiles away such negative and immature concepts, teaching us the perfect repose and joy of the spirit's confidence in *God as Love.* He enjoins radiant acquiescence as the correct response to God's Will. For more than forty years He was a prisoner and exile, but during that time He knew only happiness. I think this can only be because He lives in perfect harmony with Divine Will and with every aspect of human creation.

Such a perfect balance of spirit does not go unnoticed, but emanates like a kingly power. Perhaps this is what is meant by those people who claim to see auras. I feel sure it must be what the master painters intended in painting haloes around Holy figures. Wherever He passed, either among the sophisticated gathered in the hotel or the peasants in the countryside, eyes turned to follow and the crowds, with involuntary reverence, stood back. He is an irresistible magnet to children – they run forward to receive His blessing. One of the Persian gentlemen in His party told me that when passing through a village near Thonon, 'Abdu'l-Bahá dismounted from the carriage and walked in order to relieve the horses in a steep climb. The villagers clustered around Him, bared their heads and called Him 'Father'. One woman ran into her house and brought out some coarse bread and homemade cheese –

'Accept this, dear Father,' she said.

I pray that I shall be worthy of the blessings these days have brought me. He has bidden me show you the utmost love and obedience and to strive to become your spiritual as well as physical daughter so that you might rejoice in my distinction. That distinction, He said, must be spiritual – you must first be distinguished for your love of God and your service to humanity. When I asked about my singing He said that I should continue to study, for He hopes that we who follow Him will be distinguished in all ways. He teaches that music is a ladder by which souls may ascend to the realm on high. Surely, mamma, I cannot go wrong if I heed His advice – does it not reflect the highest hopes you and papa hold for me?

There is some hope that 'Abbás Effendi may come to America. If this comes to pass, I beg you to make an effort to see Him. Emily, I know, will be aware of His whereabouts and will be most happy to try to arrange it.

———————

Hotel du Parc
1 September 1911

Nels,

A few random thoughts before I sleep – random and probably not lucid. I cannot argue beyond my limited insight nor even clothe that pale glimmer in the rags of words. But if you could read my heart in this moment you would rejoice for me.

Beyond all our discursive reasoning and lofty speculation and wordy abstractions – beyond all that tyranny of the mind – there is a higher seriousness that leads to elation and joy and lifts us out of the ordinary mediocrity of living. I think we must fall from pride to experience it. And 'Abdu'l-Bahá compels it in one with a word or gesture. I sink into this happiness a hundred times during one hour in His presence. I say 'sink', but it is also a soaring; one sinks from pride, falls from the ordinary, to rise unfettered in an ecstasy that while rooted in the physical world yet has a trajectory in the sky. I see now more clearly than ever the truth that we cannot live our lives in compartments, that divine matters are not a round of duties and obligations separated from life but an element discernible in all circumstances and situations of living – the ignited wick in the candle. This is the truth of it. Can we not love reason and speculation greatly, but love truth more?

Nels, I am so happy I could burst. My skin feels stretched too tightly on my body to contain me. But I have never felt more alive, more connected to the beautiful earth. I see patterns and meanings in everything. A blade of grass, in this moment, has the power to speak to me of galaxies and of eternal worlds.

I am not making sense, my dear, but had to dash this off to you. It is late. Please forgive your sleepy Althea.

———

Emily, my dear,

I have almost no recollection of what I may or may not have written to you thus far, and indeed you will recognize that this divine experience is almost incommunicable and any attempt to describe it must be inadequate. These have been quiet days for the Master – no formal meetings, just small gatherings; a lovely visit to Vevey by boat; a motorcar trip with Laura and Hippolyte and Juliet – and, for us, these have been days of bliss, full of parable and symbol and tender personal touches.

Juliet is agonizing over the fact that she has been asked to prepare an account of these days for the *Star of the West*, and since both of us have moved like sleepwalkers through the experience, our eyes constantly misting, I am of little help to her in making notes. We have agreed that a kaleidoscopic report will result and perhaps serve the purpose. We are both a little awed by the realization that the visit of the Master to Thonon is the most significant event in the history of France, though the historians of today are unaware of it.

'But I'm not an historical observer, I'm an artist,' Juliet wailed. I tried to cheer her up by saying that if God had wanted an historian present, He was perfectly capable of having arranged it. 'Anyway,' I said, 'I'm sure that future generations will be grateful for your account and would not wish for a better one.'

'I suspect they'll wish I were a better speller!' Juliet retorted and returned to her notes with a sigh. She has a delicious sense of humor – no wonder you get along. She also has something of your *persistence* (ahem!) and has not lost a single opportunity to attempt to extract a promise that the Master will visit America. I think He teases her, in delight at her devotion and persistence. During one outing when we paused to admire a waterfall He asked her, eyes twinkling, if she would show Him such waterfalls if He were to go to America. She immediately launched into a description of the grandeur of Niagara Falls. Then pausing – amused at her own verbosity and recognizing the implication of what He said – she exclaimed, 'But surely Your coming does not depend upon my invitation!'

The Master was suddenly grave. 'My invitation to America will be the unity of the believers,' He said.

Oh Emily, if it comes to pass, think what it will mean to May! Could it be possible that He might reach Montreal?

Did I tell you that Miss Elizabeth Stewart and Miss Lillian Kappes were summoned to Thonon? They were in London for some weeks in hopes of seeing the Master at the Congress, but of course He was unable to be present. He therefore summoned them here and has showered the greatest bounties upon them, for within two days they are leaving for Persia to assist Dr Moody and Dr Clock.

Lillian told us of her private interview with the Master. She mentioned to Him that the hills rising beyond the lake were what she called her hills of dream and said she never expected to view them in this life. 'Sometimes the heart sees what the eyes cannot see,' the Master told her. 'If it were not for the Cause of Bahá'u'lláh we would never have met, you would not be here.' He told her that she was being sent to Persia to *serve* – stressing that – and warned her that there would be many difficulties as is always the case when we attempt to do God's bidding.

He called her to Him for a final interview, saying as she left, 'I will see you again in the Kingdom of Heaven.' Was a sadder, sweeter farewell ever taken from His presence?

Later Juliet told me that if she thought she might never live in hope of seeing the Master again in this world, she would want to die. She was close to tears and to divert her I couldn't resist saying, 'But I thought you told me He wants us to live to serve!'

'Touché!' said Juliet. And we both began to weep. At last I have learned that 'weeping for joy' is not an idle phrase.

---

c/o Miss Marion Jack
137A High Street, Kensington
5 September 1911

Dearest Maggie,

I hope you will enjoy the scenic views I am enclosing. I am enjoying London very much and am the guest of a Canadian friend who is very well acquainted with the maritime area where your brother lives, having been born in New Brunswick. She says the landscape there is awesome and ruggedly beautiful. Now I can appreciate, from her descriptions, how very much you must have enjoyed your visit to the Canadian branch of your family.

Miss Jack was an art student in Paris for some years and particularly likes to do landscape painting. She is a hearty, jolly woman and reminds me very much of you. I admire her greatly. She has something of your excellent common sense and doughty spirit. Her smile, especially, reminds me of yours; I would find it difficult to say 'No' to anything she asked if she accompanied her request with a smile. I would like to have you hear her comments on English cooking! She has lived in London for a time so is very helpful in guiding me about. It is fascinating to be surrounded again by people who speak English – at least I think that is what they speak, for the variety of accents is bedlam and some seem to speak so quickly that I cannot make out what they say, and my repeated 'Pardon me's?' must cause them to wonder whether I am deaf or just mentally backward.

I have found some marvelous yarn in an especially pretty turquoise shade – enough, I think, for a shawl for you – and will be sending it along shortly.

Please tell mamma and papa that I shall write later. As you may imagine, I am kept very busy pursuing the real purpose of this visit, a purpose towards which I feel you would be sympathetic if I could but see you and explain.

c/o Miss Marion Jack
137A High Street, Kensington
12 September 1911

Dear Nels,

Visited the Tate Gallery, and the newly-completed Turner wing. Turner's works are extraordinary renderings of the physical universe, but I had no patience for representations of clouds and mountains so in tumult is the inner landscape of my soul. Juliet Thompson and I shall return later to give Mr Turner his due, for indeed our debt to him, as to all 'masters', is significant.

———————

c/o Miss Marion Jack
137A High Street, Kensington
12 September 1911

Dearest Emily,

While I was opening my writing case a note fell out reminding me to send you, with Juliet's permission, an excerpt from her diary, written on August 28th when our days in Thonon were drawing to a close. Anticipating as He does our every hidden wish, reading the most private chambers of the heart, 'Abdu'l-Bahá drew Juliet aside and said, 'We will never be separated. I shall be with you always. You will go back to America and I may return to 'Akká, but we will be together.' He could have given her no gift that would have brought greater ease to her yearning heart. 'We *will* be together,' Juliet repeated to me

127

later, with brimming eyes. Then smiling, she said, 'Is it not so?'

But how to describe the events in London? I long to proclaim it from the rooftops that all might know – the Son of the Manifestation of God arrived on Monday, September 4th, and London lay before Him like a variegated carpet spread humbly in His welcome. Even in the hurly-burly of this vast, grey cosmopolitan metropolis He stands out like a beacon light inspiring an awed reverence in the strained faces of even its most negligent citizens of every class and rank. The friends have streamed in from various points in Europe and America. Never have I been with so many of the believers; it is a foretaste of the millennial dream of the poets, a glimpse of the universal brotherhood of man!

Alma Knobloch is here from Stuttgart with Mr and Mrs Herrigel and Mr Haiges; Mr Mountfort Mills, Mr Honore Jaxon, Mr Remey and others from America; the Paris friends; 'Jackie', of course, who is my hostess (did you know that the Master calls her 'General Jack!' – she truly has been His valiant soldier) – I could not begin to list everyone. And the splendid English Bahá'ís for whom I have the greatest admiration – Sarah Ridgeway, Arthur Cuthbert, Eric Hammond, Ethel Rosenberg, Mrs Thornburgh-Cropper, Lady Blomfield – they have an enviable stability, and great wisdom and foresight. Through their instrumentality and their intelligent efforts to support the activity of progressive leaders of thought and Christian social action, the churches and the press and various liberal and free-thinking groups have flung open their doors to the Master and to the presentation of the Bahá'í Teachings. The Master said He was *pleased* with the English believers. He told them: 'I was tired when I boarded the steamer, but when I reached London and beheld the faces of the believers, my fatigue left me. Your great love refreshes me.'

The Cause in England has no more gracious, gallant and noble worker than Lady Blomfield to whom the Master has given the name Sitárih Khánum. She has put her charming flat at 97 Cadogan Gardens at His disposal. I have made a little word-picture of His arrival there and hope to set it to music when my mind is less full of the music of His presence:

The Guest

He arrived, and who shall picture Him?
One saw, as in a clear vision,
That He had so wrought all good and mercy
That the inner grace of Him
Had grown greater than all outer sign,
And the radiance of this inner glory shone
In every glance
    and word
       and movement
As He approached with hands outstretched.
    Your love has drawn me here. I waited
    forty years in prison to bring the Message
    to you. Are you pleased to receive such a guest?

The house bulges at the seams with pilgrims, guests, visitors from every quarter of the globe, the Occident and Orient, every day, all day long,

129

a constant stream, an interminable procession, from every walk of life, from every field of human interest and endeavour, and none too lowly or too great to receive a sympathetic audience with the Harbinger of Glad-Tidings.

The Master received Archdeacon Wilberforce and accepted an invitation to speak to the congregation of St. John the Divine at Westminster on September 17th. But I forgot to say that on September 10th He gave His first public address in the West from the pulpit of the City Temple in Holborn. Never, I thought, had He looked more beautiful. One could never have imagined that He was a prisoner and exile and by the standards of the world untutored! He was kingly in His simplicity as He stood, a gracious figure clothed in purest white, in the hushed silence of the City Temple. His words must have pierced all but hearts of stone when He said: '*This is a new cycle of human power. All the horizons of the world are luminous, and the world will become indeed as a garden and a paradise. It is the hour of unity of the sons of men and of the drawing together of all races and all classes . . .* '

Miss Rosenberg leaned toward me and whispered, 'The devout of every faith have for centuries awaited such an announcement; will they listen?'

I could not help but think of papa and mamma and the distance which seems to separate them from recognition of these words.

———

c/o Miss Marion Jack
137A High Street, Kensington
13 September 1911

Dear Michael,

Horace Holley, an American poet, has given me a few of his lines:

England

I gaze upon the golden steaming hills,
England! and yield a grateful heart to thee.
What! this cottage thatched against the sun,
This April morning steeped in fallow glebe,
And not an English heart broken in rapture
To keep thee – England?
The Vandal poets wait against the coast
To conquer thee and give the land a soul.

'Abdu'l-Bahá is England's April, Michael. She needs no other nor will she ever be warmed by this April's like. And I have seen with my own unworthy eyes April's triumph and many hearts broken by the rapture of this light!

Is Paris prepared to receive her Spring?

———

c/o Miss Marion Jack
137A High Street, Kensington
14 September 1911

Dear Emily,

I am distressed to say I must return to Paris next week, and yet the Master will remain here, it is thought, until the end of the month. I would accuse myself of lacking the courage and fine madness of the saints in not abandoning my responsibilities and remaining here, if the Master had not so sweetly explained that duty and obedience are expressions of service – and service is what He asks of us. It comforts me to think that I can spread the Teachings – this He says is the *great* work – and still obey the authority of my parents and the demands of my music training. But still that is little enough consolation for the cold wave of desolation that sweeps over me when I contemplate being separated from 'Abdu'l-Bahá. But I shall see Him again in Paris and perhaps can assist, meanwhile, in the preparations for His arrival, for a great part of the responsibility for this will fall upon the shoulders of Hippolyte and Laura.

Juliet, the lucky creature, will remain to the end and come on to Paris with the Master. She is feeling better about her record of the Master's visit now that others are assisting her.

Jackie, with that deep gleeful chuckle I have come to love, offered Juliet a consoling thought *apropos* her not being a historian yet being called upon to be one of the recording amanuenses for posterity, as it were, reminding her that the Master said, in effect, that most of what has been written by the most learned of European and American historians regarding Muḥammad has been utter falsehood, and that Juliet's account, however inadequate, would at least be a true and eyewitness report. Juliet grimaced and said she thought historians would be more objective than she, but was obviously not displeased. Irrepressible Juliet! Still, she mused later, what would we not give to have one uncorrupted report of some aspect of the early events of Christianity? And then: But with the Master in our midst, what need have we to congratulate ourselves on our good fortune? Let's enjoy it!

Juliet, I probably need not add, persists in her efforts to persuade the Master to visit America, mentioning what it would mean to the friends to have Him visit and dedicate the Mashriqu'l-Adhkár and bless the Annual Convention with His presence. (You probably know she has a burning desire to paint His portrait though dares not mention it and indeed says she cannot imagine how a mere human hand could sketch that noble head.)

I had a few private moments with dear Alma Knobloch and welcomed the opportunity of getting to know her. Her dedication is most admirable. She says that the visit of our distinguished Negro brother from America, Mr Louis Gregory, to various centers in Germany last spring produced astonishing results. He is a man of great intelligence, eloquence, integrity and personal charm and the Stuttgart believers have received from the Master a wonderful Tablet in tribute to his services. He was with 'Abdu'l-Bahá in Alexandria in April and visited the Shrines in the Holy Land before coming on to Europe. Alma said that Mr Gregory literally throbbed with light and life. The Master wrote that he is a new creation, a manifestor of the graces of the world of humanity, and that he shines as a bright light. We could all wish to be deserving of such praise from the lips of our Loved One.

I have scarcely thought of Paris since I left – it seems remote and unreal in the light of the events of these past days which have a celestial and compelling reality. But today I found myself thinking that surely the visit of 'Abdu'l-Bahá will be the means of winning Nels and Michael to the Faith. Even if they were made of wood, how could they resist the Divine Kindler of Hearts? But still, the Master reminds us that many are called and few are chosen – and how many, many meanings lie enfolded in those words! 'Why us?' my heart cries out? 'Why should we have been gifted with "eyes to see and ears to hear"? Where are the noble and good and learned and wise and deserving? What veils obscure them from this manifest light?' Not that the celebrated do not seek out the Master and show respect, but how many of them will be His instruments? So many are doing the work of the Kingdom in one way or another – I think of Mrs Emmeline Pankhurst, the suffragist, for instance – but how few there are who recognize the source, and most of those unacclaimed.

Juliet and I were speaking today of young Thomas Breakwell – you will remember that we heard from May's own lips the story of that young Englishman; Juliet, of course, knew him too from her early days in Paris. What a rare soul he must have been, and how consecrated his love for the Cause, and yet by all the standards of the world his was a wasted existence; in their eyes he must be considered but one of 'the nameless and traceless poor.' Now that I have met the English friends I feel I must visit Breakwell's grave in Paris on their behalf and place flowers there – violets, Juliet said, would symbolize perfectly his fragile beauty and sweetness of soul. His spirit must be gladdened by the visit of the Master to England. I enclose for you a translation of the Master's eulogy which I shall recite over his grave (though perhaps you already have a copy). I am told the Master wept as He dictated the words; and certainly I cannot recite it without tears: '*O Breakwell, my beloved! Where is thy beautiful countenance . . .*'

Tender thoughts of you and Peter fill my mind frequently and I close each day with a prayer for your happiness. When are you getting married? I hope to find a nice fat letter awaiting me on my return to Paris.

———

c/o Miss Marion Jack
137A High Street, Kensington
14 September 1911

Dear Michael,

I lose my heart to Him every day. Had He not departed a gathering by pressing into the hands of the friends tufts of unassuming heartsease plucked by His own hands from a small domestic garden, my heart would not have shattered this past twenty-four hours. But each day brings its own dissolving gesture against which I am without defences.

135

If you will bear with me I shall tell you much more upon my return.

————

c/o Miss Marion Jack
137A High Street, Kensington
14 September 1911

Dear Maggie,

These petals will fade as this letter leaves my hand, but take their bruised form to your lips and kiss them, for they came from the hand of my Beloved, and I think must carry a special blessing which I yearn to have you share.

Beside your bed you keep your well-thumbed Bible; will you press these petals between its pages in memory of me?

————

c/o Miss Marion Jack
137A High Street, Kensington
14 September 1911

Dear Ada and Paul,

I have been unable to assimilate the events of the past days sufficiently to write of them in any coherent way; I think their telling must await our next meeting. But my brain is still functioning to the extent that I could not let the opportunity pass of obtaining some suit lengths of very fine tweed which I am packaging off to you, together with some small surprises for the children. The whole is wrapped in my love. You have been constantly in my thoughts and I have resolved to find a way to share with you the nectar of these past days. Till I am able to do so, please let this promise sustain you.

———

Paris
25 September 1911

Dear Emily,

A note in haste to say that I returned safely and found your nice long letter which I promise to answer soon. Although I feel severed from the very source of life and am depressed by what I can only describe as the 'greyness' of life here in what now seems a stale and flat existence, I am cheered by the thought that the Master soon will illumine the dullness of Paris through His presence on the soil of France. I am cheered, too, by a new-found courage in seizing opportunities to speak about the Faith among the students at the Conservatory and the most casual of acquaintances. Perhaps my 'pilgrimage' has changed me, opened channels for the attraction of the Holy Spirit – I cannot say. Possibly these opportunities always existed and I have simply developed a heightened sensitivity to them. In any case, I have just to recall the Master's face and I find that the power to speak of the Cause, as well as the opportunity, is given me.

Michael had been in touch with some of the Paris friends and was at the station to meet me on my return. He has plied me with questions and listens to my answers with close attention, but whether he does so through courtesy and affection, or in his own right, for his own soul's feasting, I am not sure. He wants very much to meet 'Abdu'l-Bahá and you may be sure it will be arranged.

Nels has called by, too, of course and asked about the Master – he even suggested he might interview 'Abdu'l-Bahá for the purpose of writing a profile or a series of articles – but once I had agreed to speak to Hippolyte who could arrange it, he dropped the subject and has not referred to it again. I have not tried to press the matter because, as May told us, the cup must first be empty. So I let Nels talk – he is full of his book these days – and he seems grateful for my attention. He has a great need for a sympathetic, patient and attentive ear, and for the moment that may be the greatest service I can render him.

––––––––––

Paris
27 September 1911

Emily, dear,

I was startled by your letter today and the thought that your young friend, Henry, should have fallen in love with you. The manner in which you and Peter treated the matter has greatly impressed me. I am afraid I should have blundered along growing increasingly confused, and probably should have hurt Henry's feelings cruelly. He sounds like a sincere young man and very sensitive. But how alarming to have attempted to open the door of the Revelation for him and to have found yourself blocking his entry because of his misdirected devotion. I had not considered before how closely our teaching activities resemble a romantic relationship and how easily the hungering heart can confuse his feeling toward the gift with those he experiences for the giver. No doubt it is, as Peter explained, that never before had Henry been the object of such marked attention and disinterested love – certainly not from a young woman as beautiful and vibrant as you – and his response was a natural one, to feel that he was in love with you. Since the language of the lower emotions, not to say of the flesh, is the first we learn, it is all too easy to translate our first spiritual awakening into those terms. I'm glad that the three of you have resolved the problem in a way that causes Henry no embarrassment, and that he continues to come round to study the Teachings. I agree with you – for a while you should avoid being alone with him.

Perhaps in saying this I throw light on my own ineptitude in my treatment of Nels – but I had no Peter to confer with. Still, I do not forget that your immediate response to my relationship with Nels was tinged with distrust. I longed for him to have the light of the Faith, but my own shadow has obscured it from him. Now he will have the chance to enter the presence of the Master Who is all light and casts no shadow, and surely my candle will be so dwarfed by the sun of 'Abdu'l-Bahá's greatness that all will come clear for Nels and he will see only the eternal horizon, unending and unblemished, and know that the attraction he felt for me was really an attraction for the Teachings and my dim mirroring of them. I must break off before this metaphor carries me even further beyond the realm of sense, and because I must prepare for another meeting at which the Master will again speak to us. I think of the time He spends with us as the children's hour; He generously indulges us as a kind father might. I gather never-fading memories from these days of belated childhood.

Paris
28 September 1911

Dearest Ada and Paul,

Your most welcome letter arrived and brought me happiness. Yes, mamma was correct in saying that there is a strong possibility that 'Abbás Effendi may visit America soon, and I shall certainly let you know when details are settled. You will derive great pleasure and benefit from meeting Him, I am sure, and to do so will assist you to understand why Emily and I are so deeply affected by the Bahá'í Teachings.

I enclose a lengthy article from the *Christian Commonwealth* of September 13th – an interview between 'Abbás Effendi and Rev R. J. Campbell – as well as a few random clippings describing 'Abdu'l-Bahá's visit to London. I hope these will interest you. Surely His remarks about the need for universal spiritual unity seem especially timely in view of the Agadir crisis and the mounting tension in Italy. How far removed seem such events from the ideal world He describes as the goal towards which our leaders should devote their resources and energies. I had never seen sorrow on His face until I heard Him refer to these matters, as though He saw the horizon of Europe threatened by dark and ominous clouds beyond our sight. It was the sorrow one might see in a parent watching helplessly a wilful child blindly running towards a dangerous precipice. And never have I had such an experience of my own powerlessness. I could think of nothing I might do that could lift from His holy face that burden of sorrow for humanity.

I barely have time for classes these days but Prof Clémenceau, like an angelic walrus, twitches his dear face into a huge smile and tells me to follow my heart. 'Later you will translate this experience into music,' he said.

———

Paris
18 October 1911

My dear Emily,

I feel I have neglected you shamefully but you will understand that these days have been full of both frenzied activity and divine calm, as I have swung like a pendulum between the demands of my outer world and the timeless bliss of that other reality when in the Master's presence. And so much to tell you!

Let me begin with Michael Athlone. He was given an audience with the Master and in simplest terms went in like a lion and came out like a lamb. Not that he was hostile or aggressive, but I could tell that he had carefully buckled on his intellectual armor and was intending to be a respectful but dispassionate and objective observer. He emerged with the radiance of a child who has been favored by his grandfather, and came towards me seizing my hand warmly. 'There are no words for Him,' he said softly, and I knew in that instant that my hand was being clasped by a fellow believer; though Michael says he needs time before committing himself to the Cause. And since then it has not been possible to keep him from any opportunity of glimpsing the Master, however briefly. Michael's warm brown eyes glow with a new tenderness and not infrequently are seen to brim. I realized once again that I have never seen my father cry and I regret that Western men should have been trained to consider tears an inappropriate response to moments that might call forth these 'pearls of the spirit'.

Once Michael exclaimed to me, 'Why didn't you *tell* me!' – (as though I had ever kept silent about the Cause if given the slightest opportunity!) – and then seeing my face which must have been a study in perfect astonishment he burst out laughing in which I spontaneously joined, and we ran along the street giggling like children in a manner that would cause Bostonian eyebrows to lift – at one time, I suppose, my own.

Did Juliet tell you in her letters from London that while 'Abdu'l-Bahá was in England He spent a weekend in Bristol at Clifton Guest House? A wonderful reception was tendered Him with almost one hundred notables of Bristol in attendance – arranged, I suppose, with the assistance of Mr Tudor-Pole. And the Master's last address in London was on September 30th at the new headquarters of the Theosophical Society – Mrs Annie Besant, the president of the movement, having extended the invitation. Perhaps you have also heard of the attack on 'Abdu'l-Bahá made by Rev Peter Z. Easton in the *English Churchman*. How tragic and ill-informed! And yet a warning for us that attacks will be forthcoming, no doubt from various quarters and undreamed-of sources.

Indeed, I have had a small personal glimpse of this (though not comparable, of course) about which I shall tell you presently. I'm sorry to say it involved Nels. His book is progressing and he has been elated because of Michael's firm's interest in publishing it, and so is working hard to bring his book to completion. I have wondered whether he is premature in his optimism, for the publishing house may not accept the book when it is in final form, but Nels acts as though it were *un fait accompli* and has been ebullient every time we met. In addition, he has sold a number of articles and reviews and this has bolstered his confidence. He has been completely at ease with me these past weeks and, although we rarely talk about the Cause, he has eagerly discussed his work and has developed a mild appreciation of Michael's poems

– though he feels that Michael is a better editor and anthologist than poet. It was all the more surprising, therefore, that he should have suddenly turned on me – I might say almost savagely.

We had had dinner in the Quarter, strolled along the boulevard on Mont Parnasse, bantering lightly, and then when we reached my door, he attempted to force himself upon me with a frightening intensity. When I withdrew with a sharp exclamation he seized my arm bruisingly and attempted to compel me to kiss him, tearing my sleeve in the process. As calmly as I could, I asked him to leave, but he flew into a rage and accused me of rejecting him for Michael because of Michael's interest in the Cause. It was an angry and incoherent torrent, but incongruously his face was pale and tight, and his blue eyes were like ice, glazed with rage. Ridiculously, I found myself perfectly controlled and the irrelevant thought strayed into my mind, 'Poor Nels, his blond hair is thinning and he will be quite bald before he is forty. How vulnerable he is!'

And then, almost without pausing for breath, he launched into an attack on me – asserting that I am a spoiled, hysterical and deluded woman, a simpering missionary, puritanically repressing my normal desires, incapable of recognizing that my interest in a pseudo-religion springs from my adolescent refusal to accept life as it is; that the Bahá'í Faith is a heretical sect of the Moslem Faith, a kind of Moslem gnosticism, born of a power struggle between grasping members of a divided Persian family; that it is little better than an eclectic philosophy now being peddled in a new guise suited to the naive and gullible Western mind; that the Bahá'í women are pampered socialites playing charades, adopting head veils and Persian names and toying with learning the language, mesmerized by the personality of the Master – and on and on and on.

It could not have been uglier nor more vicious, and just at the point when I found it unbearable and might have burst into tears or screamed denial, I saw what was happening – I saw the terror in Nels' soul and realized that the attack was not directed at me at all. It was like gazing into the eyes of a trapped animal whose life is at stake. And I was instantly flooded with relief, for then I knew that Nels at last has been brought face to face with the challenge of the Cause. His soul is like a threatened citadel and all that he said was a defence against that threat, a desperate grasping at straws, a throwing up of elaborate fortifications of will and intellect and ego. He really is fighting for his life. At least now he may be free to choose the Cause or reject it in full knowledge of what he is doing. Now, more than ever, I realize I must be kind, must help him to see what he is doing, and somehow work out my own response to his panic in a manner that accords with the Bahá'í principles. Not that I know what principles apply! But I think of the injunction that one must reject the sin but not the sinner, that one must be a refuge for the fugitive, and so on. Nels seems to be a fugitive from his own reality.

When Nels subsided I spoke as evenly as I could, constantly repeating the Greatest Name in my mind, begging to be guided to the right words. When I turned to go, he had tears in his eyes. 'Don't abandon me,' he pleaded, and he began to apologize, choking back sobs. I thought it wise to say no more than that I would try to be his friend. He begged to see me again and I consented, for I feel it would be cruel to bring things to an end on such a bitter note. It is strange to reflect that he would really want to see me again, if he really believed all he said about me and the Cause – proof, I think, that I interpreted correctly the reason for his fear.

Now I understand my reservation about accepting Nels' earlier declarations of love. I always felt that he didn't know me. It is himself he doesn't know, so how can he know anyone else? But if he is now beginning to look within, if he can find the courage to turn and do battle with his lower self and slay his inner dragons, he will have taken the most courageous step it is possible for a human being to take. The victory over the lower self is what engages all who seek the Promised One, as May so often told us, but what a lonely task it is! None to take up the battle for us, and victory not won conclusively until our last breath! On darker days I think it all seems unfair. But anyway, we can at least cheer one another on from the sidelines. It is what is at stake in this battle that I think Nels has finally seen. Oh Emily, I can never forget his look of sheer terror.

Michael chides me, rather than sympathizes – that is, when he lets down the barrier behind which he nurses his private burden (or is it a gift he hugs to his chest and will not share?). 'Althea,' he said when I first spoke to him about my disturbing experience with Nels, 'has it occurred to you that you are attracted to Nels' weakness; that you could possibly marry him in order to enjoy holding him in contempt, using that as an excuse for abandoning him to freely devote yourself to Bahá'í work? You both deserve something better than that. If you can, let the man go.'

I never felt more naked and ashamed, but his tone was so tender and solicitous and his gaze so warm with concern that I could not take offence. Seeing that I was fighting back tears, he took my hand and pressed it until I was in control.

'I'm sorry, I had no right to say that,' he said.

I was sincere when I replied, 'I needed to hear it. Thank you for telling me to grow up.'

We walked home slowly and in silence, and I kept glancing sideways at Michael wondering what impulse caused him to speak as he did, and reflecting that kindness takes many forms. I truly want Nels to be free enough of me to make that lonely and courageous choice we all must make. But in some small corner of my *self* I realize I would basely like to chain him to my will. How complex is the human heart!

Paris
12 November 1911

Dear Maggie,

I was grieved by the fact that you should have

147

had to write as you did, but touched by the kind impulse that prompted your doing so. 'Antichrist' is a word I had hoped would never be found on the lips of my father in relation to Bahá'u'lláh Whose birth we are celebrating today; and that papa should have, in rage, flung that shocking title at Paul and Ada in the presence of the children and mamma and yourself, I know must have upset you even more deeply than your letter suggested. I know that you will try to understand, as I must also try, that papa is alarmed by the study Paul and Ada are making of the Bahá'í Teachings and is concerned that they might make a grave spiritual error. Your letter confirms for me the judgment he has made of my own life's course, a judgment with which he has not yet found it possible to confront me. He is a devoted servant of God, as you know, and it is natural that his love for his children might cause him to pronounce such a verdict without having stopped to consider its truth or falsehood. I pray that his love for his family is such that he will fully investigate the Bahá'í Teachings, if only to try to rescue Paul and Ada and me if he deems us in error in accepting them; perhaps his study will clear away any prejudices or superstitions that cloud his understanding.

I do not know what papa has been reading. There are those who circulate unfounded speculation and untruths and calumnies about the Bahá'í Faith – some through misguided information, innocently but in ignorance, and some with full awareness. Where there is light, there is shadow – as I need not say.

148

As to your question whether Bahá'u'lláh is the Antichrist, I can only say that no one but you can answer that question. All I can do – certainly from this distance – is enclose a few small brochures outlining the Bahá'í Teachings and ask you to study them for yourself. I do not think you will quarrel with the basic principles enunciated by Bahá'u'lláh, that the one God has spoken to the one human race down through history through His chosen Spiritual Educators; that the great religions of the past are like chapters in one great book in which mankind's destiny is unfolded; that man must search freely after truth and not blindly accept his inherited traditions; that extremes of wealth and poverty must be eliminated; that compulsory education must be available to all; that work performed in the spirit of service is exalted to the rank of worship; that equal opportunities and rights and privileges must be granted to both men and women; that science and religion must work hand in hand for a better world – and so on. If Christ were to return, would you not expect Him to utter such words?

Read the words of Bahá'u'lláh and listen to your own heart's response. I do not think you will be deceived. Try to put His Teachings into effect in your life and observe the results. Use the prayers He has revealed and see if you find your spirit uplifted and your heart illumined. Pray to have the truth revealed to you. And use your excellent mind to think about all that you read. More I cannot say. But promise me that if after doing all these things you are convinced that this Cause is evil, you will rise up against it with all your powers and strive to put it down. Surely that is what Christ would have His true followers do, just as He would bid them give their whole beings to this Cause if it were really the renewal and fulfilment of His Cause, if it were born of the 'Spirit of Truth' promised in the Latter Days. You must not be swayed by papa telling you that this is the work of the Antichrist (for he has not examined it) nor by my telling you it is the eternal religion of God renewed (for we are taught that one's faith cannot be conditioned by another).

It seems to me that if we decide against the Bahá'í Faith and work to thwart its growth, and have made the wrong choice, we will be forgiven if our belief was sincere. God might even protect us, for all our striving will come to nothing. If this is the Cause of God it cannot be defeated by human efforts. But each of us must examine it and make his own choice.

I shall of course write to Paul and Ada – please do not feel I shall betray your confidence in doing so – and say to them very much the same thing I've said to you. No doubt they would hesitate to embarrass me by writing about the scene with papa. I am so grateful that you let me know. And I shall exert the greatest care in writing to mamma and papa in order not to aggravate this painful situation.

So glad you like the wool! What have you decided to make from it? The more fashionable French ladies are wearing mufflers this season, long affairs resembling feather boas, with great fluffy tassels at the ends. More ornamental than practical, as they are always getting caught on things – rather like strolling about with a huge string of sausages trailing after you. I choose more modest impediments but permit myself a muff of rather grand proportions.

May I commission you to step up your bullying of mamma and papa on the theme of their not over-taxing themselves at Noel? Do write and tell me what preparations are being made for Christmas.

Paris
25 November 1911

Dearest Emily,

. . . So that is the situation at home. Paul in his methodical way is reading everything he can lay his hands on, but he makes it clear that his motive is to qualify himself to rescue me from Bahá'í influences if he decides I have fallen into error. I think none of this would have come about if it were not for papa's antipathy towards the Faith, which he has not yet expressed to me. Even Ada's interest in the Faith would not likely have caused Paul to really examine it. Paul is very conventional at heart and has built his life in the Christian community, but he accepted Christianity as part of his inheritance, like his white skin and copper hair, a family accident of birth, and was never in any personal sense interested in matters of religion; he was perhaps embarrassed even to speak of such things. In his view such unmanly interests are left to women, like diapers and washing dishes, unless one is 'in the profession' like papa. But we know that a conscious spiritual life is open to everyone to experience, if he will but choose it. And Paul is very fair – if he decides for the Faith, he will be wholehearted and unswerving in its service. Ada, I think, knows the reality of the Faith – has known it from the beginning – and is merely now awaiting Paul's decision. It will so enrich their lives if they can enter it hand in hand. But I try to do as the Teachings say – remain detached from their choice. Ours the task of offering the gift!

Nels has been angelic these past weeks and making every effort to please me. Which rather worries me, in fact – I think his motive is to please *me* and to satisfy his own pride in his idealism. I wish I were convinced that his efforts were the spontaneous outflowing of his heart's response to the spirit of the Cause. Naturally, he is filled with remorse about his behavior towards me in that nasty episode I wrote to you about, and he is almost childlike in seeking to compensate for it. I never mention it, of course, other than indirectly in an attempt to have him face what I am sure is the meaning of that event. But he has a glib capacity for picking up the pieces and going on without, it seems to me, incorporating into his life the lesson, the essence, of experiences. It is as though the deeper waters of his being are sealed off and only on the surface does the ripple register the cast pebble; but I know the ripples are the merest part of it, for the stone will sink to rest somewhere in the soul.

I said he was angelic. He has written and had

published several fine pieces about the Master's visit, for which I am of course extremely grateful. But when I expressed appreciation for this he stabbed me to the quick with the words, 'I did it for *you*.' Emily, will he never learn? In that moment I felt that he was lost to me forever.

And the worst was yet to come. He was privileged to be alone with the Master and you can imagine how I anticipated the outcome. I couldn't read the mask of his face and he made no comment of any significance when he came from 'Abdu'l-Bahá's presence. Finally, I could stand it no longer. Nels was enumerating the various celebrities who had been drawn to the Master and evaluating their reaction. Impetuously and without a trace of wisdom or discretion I charged upon Nels, oblivious to the panic I had seen in him earlier. 'But what did you think of Him?' I blurted. Nels shattered me with his answer. 'Well, my dear, He is a kind, saintly and very tired old man, but He has nothing new to say. He is as anachronistic as an Old Testament Prophet. I respect Him, of course. But I think he under-estimates the social progress of man and is utterly out of touch with Western thought.'

And so I saw that Nels had lost his battle. His soul has gone down before his intellect and is safely imprisoned behind a wall of rationalization. The ripples lap and the pebble lies unnoticed at the bottom. Nels has succeeded in persuading himself it has not been cast; he has willed it so.

I learn, too, the hard lesson that the sceptical ego and proud intellect must solve their own problems in their own way, and that spirit never forces itself upon the individual but must be invited. Of what use is the intellect unless illumined by spirit – doesn't it remain a wickless lamp? 'Abdu'l-Bahá could so easily express His spiritual power to win spiritual allegiance, but He knows – how well the Master knows! – that the individual must make his own inner preparation. Our spiritual receptivity, it seems, conditions the degree of blessings we receive from Him. But even in appearing to stand in judgment of Nels I cannot truthfully say I know whether he fails himself or whether I fail him, or whether one is right to brood about these things. It is just that I would like, just once, to see Nels severed from those mechanisms by which he distances himself from life – see him flooded with intensity and passion and enthusiasm, and not those little flashes of short-lived excitement he feels for the passing notions that capture his attention; see him integrated and whole and truly happy.

———————

Paris
28 November 1911

Beloved May,

You have been so much in my heart and mind these past fleeting weeks that I cannot resist any longer the impulse to write you. How wonderfully has the Master crowned your efforts by His visit to Paris and I mourn that you could not be here to witness the sweetness and majesty of His sojourn on this soil, the nourishing outpouring of love He lavished on the saplings sprung from the seeds of your teaching here but a decade ago. France will realize one day that this bounty was drawn to her through you. Your heart must be overjoyed by the announcement, news of which I am sure has reached you, that the Master *will* come to America in the early part of next spring. Juliet has been unable to contain herself since it has been known, and Emily is ecstatic.

So few days remain of the Master's visit here. He is expected to return to Egypt on December 1st. I can bear the thought of separation from Him only by concentrating on the realization that He will be able to rest in a gentle climate in preparation for His journey to the West, and by recognizing that the friends in America will rejoice in His visit. I am even hatching a scheme, delicious to contemplate, which might result in my being able to be there to join the believers who will welcome Him. If I scheme shamelessly enough I might be able to join His ship at some point *en route*. But so much hinges on my father's health; I may be summoned home momentarily, for mamma has written that papa has had another heart attack. My parents grow increasingly antagonistic to the Faith and I must somehow find a way of building a bridge across this chasm before it is no longer possible to do so. They do not confront me with open disapproval of my Bahá'í activity – I think they fear I might make a hasty marriage as a means of obtaining my freedom, and they have pinned rather more hope than I have upon the idea that I shall have a career in music.

Emily is supremely happy. Her last letters have been full of her wedding plans. After January 5th I shall have to accustom myself to thinking of her as Mrs Peter Alderton. How much has happened since you first met us – two chattering magpies without the wisdom to have known the secret of the attraction we felt for you! How patient you were with us.

I sometimes think I have made little progress since you pointed out the path to us and I find new obstacles to spiritual growth with every step – the obstacles, of course, springing from my self (or selves!). Only recently have I solved the riddle of the crone-queen who has recurred in my dreams, a despicable, repulsive creature who imprisons innocent victims and laughs hideously at their anguished cries to be released. A chance remark of Mr Holley's, that all the images inhabiting our dreams are aspects of the self, caused me to recognize the crone-queen as a symbol of my unconquered, underground nature, a need of mine to bind people to *me* rather than allowing them the freedom to bind themselves to the Cause. So I must challenge the hag and subdue her if I am to be a pure instrument of the spirit. I have had sufficient experience in teaching to have grown alarmed at the subtle way one comes to think of the impersonal power of the Cause as being one's own personal power. The mind does not countenance the idea, so the ego proceeds undetected in its insidious and evil course, underground, as it were. My blood runs cold to think of the consequences of the danger this presents.

Possibly Nels has been the prisoner of my crone-queen self. I must release him and release myself from the need to make him my thrall. God forgive me if I have unwittingly connived at and enjoyed his dependency upon me. Released, he may never embrace the Faith but he will at least be free to work out his destiny independently without my exacting of him an adulation that feeds my vanity.

As for Michael Athlone, I shall, as the Master bids, 'Walk with him a year'; but I truly feel he is already a Bahá'í fellow-worker, totally independent of me. Wise, wise Michael recognized the crone-queen and avoided her allurement. In time, if our friendship continues to develop, I feel I would marry him if he asked me. How simple it all is, after all. One thinks for a long time that one might die of loneliness and desire, or must pine in splendid isolation awaiting the fairy-tale prince, or desperately wrench from fate the stuff from which one might hammer out in sullen wilfulness a personal destiny and happiness, and then one sees quite clearly that the foundations on which one might build a marriage are the qualities and virtues manifested in a friend whose goals are the same as one's own, one with whom one could serve side by side in the vineyard of God, given to each other in marriage, a trust from the Beloved, for the perfecting of each other's souls.

Forgive me for rambling like this, but I have never been able to restrain myself with you. I wanted to add that I sometimes feel helpless before Michael's beauty – he turns his warm eyes towards me or flicks back his straying, intractable forelock in a characteristic gesture, and my heart melts; and I think I should want him if I had to do so in defiance of God, my faith and my family. But I read a danger there. And there is the other part of it – his goodness. He has an effortless kindness that asks neither recognition nor praise; it is as undiscriminating as sunlight. I am even more powerless before that; I love his *goodness*. We can all train our voices to sing but not all are given the gift of perfect pitch; Michael's goodness is rather like that, a gift. And yet he often conceals himself from me and from others behind that polished civility. Oh May! You will have decided by now that the magpie has not learned to desist from chattering.

Beatrice Irwin, a splendid and intrepid young woman (a friend of Laura's), has been drawn to the Cause during the Master's visit. She will, I am sure, be an outstanding maidservant. She is attractive and has a brilliant mind. She's been studying electrical illumination in Paris but she has many other interests; already she has achieved some recognition for her poetry and as an actress. Michael and Nels have asked to see her work.

But again I am rambling on, resisting placing on paper what your heart must be aching for, news of the Master. I am afraid that to record His visit in any satisfactory manner is beyond my power and the attempt brings home to me with excruciating clarity the brevity of His nine weeks here and His imminent departure.

This much is easy to say: at last we have a photograph of the Master that is worthy of Him! Succumbing to our frequent pleas, and reminding us that a photograph focuses undue attention on the personality which, as you know, was never His purpose – I think He said something to the effect that if the friends insist on having photographs they should at least have good ones – He sat for Boissonnas and Taponier and selected from the photographic proofs a marvelous portrait that depicts something I have only occasionally guessed at before. In some degree it reflects His station as the Servant, but it has a quality beyond that – Emily would be able to describe it – some aspect of His Holy Essence, Bahá'u'lláh's trust and covenant in our midst.

As for the rest, a blissful series of gatherings, some intimate and tender, some in crowded congresses attended by leading figures. And running like a golden thread connecting all His days here, a motley and unending procession of humanity to the salon of the suite at No. 4 Avenue de Camoëns. Hippolyte has been a mainstay – gracious, charming, smoothing the way, providing impeccable translations. Lady Blomfield and her two daughters have rendered invaluable aid and are taking faithful notes.

I shall not soon forget the scenes I have witnessed – the Master strolling in the Trocadéro Gardens; addressing gatherings in the Theosophical Society headquarters, at *L'Alliance Spiritualiste,* in *Foyer de l'Ame*; or, having addressed a congregation of the poor in a mission hall, being escorted through a noisy throng by a towering ruffian waggling over his head a huge loaf of bread, like a homely scepter, clearing a passage for the Master and calling to the rowdy crowd, 'Make way! Make way! He is my Father!' some part of the man's soul having instantly responded to his first glimpse of the Master at the edge of the boisterous mob. That wonderful gift of instantaneous recognition – how few have it!

One sought His presence who had devoted sixteen years to working in the French Congo for the relief of the hardships of the native people, and was told, 'It was a great comfort to Me in the darkness of My prison to know the work you were doing.' My heart leapt to realize the comfort it must bring the Master to know of your efforts in Canada, so much more closely related to spreading the Glad-Tidings, for I have not forgotten what you said, that all who work for the good of humanity perform the work of the Kingdom, but that it is the Bahá'ís who are privileged to have the blueprint for the erection of the dam that will stop the flood which threatens to engulf mankind.

The day He arrived in London, 'Abdu'l-Bahá said, 'Heaven has blessed this day' – but I think we are far from understanding in what measure His sojourn in the West has been a benefit to the world. Mr Holley, whose creative and original mind I admire, when we were discussing this matter, I felt described accurately the difference between the London and Paris visits when he said that in London the Master emphasized the social and spiritual aspects of the Bahá'í Faith and in Paris He revealed its intellectual content and unparalleled power of definition.

'But what will His journey to America unfold?' I asked.

Mr Holley looked thoughtful, then said, 'I think the Bahá'ís are being prepared for a great undertaking – Bahá'u'lláh's universal system or order that will be the reflection on earth of the Kingdom of God, its mirror-image, not a place of harps and angels and golden streets but an elevated social order raised up by ordinary humans who suffer and love and struggle and achieve. The little Bahá'í communities of the world are like musicians who have been mastering their instruments, but this cannot continue forever. Soon the Conductor will take the podium and with His divine baton call upon them to play in symphony.'

'A Masterwork,' Michael volunteered; and then fearing that we might have thought he punned, he added, 'God's Supreme Masterwork'.

But none had misunderstood.

———

Paris
28 December 1911

Dear Mamma,

Your Christmas letter arrived and brought great happiness, and how shall I thank you for the beautiful gift? If you knew how much I have longed for a pair of really splendid opera glasses you could gauge my surprise and gratitude. Maggie's fruitcake arrived intact, and you may tell her that it was shared only with the most deserving among my ravenous friends.

I am sorry that my visit to England took place

before aunt Edna's arrival there. Perhaps we can persuade her to visit me here before she returns to Vermont. It is unlikely that I shall be able to interrupt my studies to meet her in London, as Prof Clémenceau, having smiled upon my frequent absences of late, now urges me to concentrate.

A quiet Christmas was spent here. I went with friends – Laura and Hippolyte whom I've surely mentioned before – and Michael Athlone – to a Debussy recital by Maggie Teyte, the composer himself accompanying her. Miss Teyte is as lovely as her voice; I glimpse how far I am from realizing Prof Clémenceau's ambitions for me. She has a unique capacity to enter deeply into the spirit of the songs and of interpreting them impeccably. Later there was a small gathering at Prof C's, its merriment impoverished by Emily's absence, and my own power to enter into the festivities a little dimmed by homesickness. Increasingly my thoughts turn back to America and I sometimes feel I shall have no peace until I return. Perhaps the real purpose of my coming to Paris has already been achieved and my attendance at the Conservatory was merely one in a chain of circumstances. Do not be distressed by this rambling – I am merely talking aloud about a decision I feel increasingly impelled to make.

Hug everyone for me and wish them a happy New Year.

I have made a little song which Prof Clémenceau has praised. I hope papa will like it. It remains for me to complete the refrain and attempt a French translation. I have not yet proceeded beyond '*mon cœur est un oiseau peureux*':

My heart is a frightened bird
Trembling in the small cage of my breast.
Not until your honeyed voice is heard
Will the frail and feathered tenant come to rest.
Then speak, my Love, and coax the bird to peace;
At your sweet accents only will it sing
And flee the cold, rude bars in glad release
To astound remoteness in a flash of wing.

I wanted the first line to read 'My heart is a tiny frightened bird' but Michael said that sounds too precious. I was gratified that he liked the verse.

You may think it strange that I have been thinking of the theme of 'remoteness' and 'separation' these past weeks, but with the departure of 'Abdu'l-Bahá from Paris a sense of loneliness descended on me, and everything has seemed overcast, as though He took with Him the very sky with its sun and moon and stars – a feeling more unbearable than homesickness or the absence of friends and family. Divine ecstasy such as I have known exacts heavy dues. I wish you and papa were here to comfort me.

———————

Paris
15 January 1912

Dear Emily and Peter,

Forgive me, darling Emily, that I have not written and cannot write to you about the

Master's leaving Paris, a foretaste of death. Your own leave-taking of Him when your pilgrimage ended, about which you could never speak without weeping, is the explanation. My diary is mute on this subject for which there are no words. I cling to His thought that in the realm of the spirit there is no separation; perhaps if I had 'met' Him on that plane more fully, I would not feel as though a cruel hand had snatched away the light of day. But all of this is experienced only in the human realm. In another sense His coming into our midst was a calling us to life, revitalizing us to live lives of an order higher than we have known. He took with Him more than His physical presence but also the ordinary mediocrity of our existence. Another meaning of 'the Lord giveth and He taketh away?' Heaven matches earth in presenting us with paradoxes. I suppose this is reasonable, if the world is truly heaven's image, though earth's glass is cloudy and distorting.

Thinking of you in your new life has helped me ease my way into acceptance of the Master's departure, as has the realization that change and flow and growth are essentially spiritual laws. It came to me that the Cause is a wave, a great universal timeless wave through which we pass, all of us single drops of the wave. Watching the beautiful figure of 'Abdu'l-Bahá take His leave from us, he appeared to withdraw and diminish like a fading echo or the last rays of sunlight, and I saw His deep fatigue and realized that He would one day leave His earthly temple – I had never quite dared face the idea of His death before. And however deep a blow that will be to those of us who love Him, the Cause, I know, will endure – for the Master is not the Cause. However great His station, He too is part of the great wave, as we are parts of it, individual drops each contributing to the force of the wave, swept across the universe and deposited on the far shore of the after-life; and with or without us the wave released by Bahá'-u'lláh's coming will continue, constantly gathering force and momentum and power as new drops are added. The disaffected will be cast off as foam, and the wave, undulating in God's eternal rhythm, will be purified and will roll on resistlessly to flood the parched earth with life-giving water.

I suppose you know that Alice Beede and Mary Hanford Ford were with us during 'Abdu'l-Bahá's visit? In addition, some of the friends from Stuttgart were able to be present for a few days – Mr and Mrs Eckstein, Mr and Mrs Häfner and their son, Otto, Miss Margarethe Döring, and a few others. They had hoped to persuade the Master to visit Germany but it was not possible. He did, however, before leaving Paris dictate a Tablet for the German friends which Lady Blomfield has promised to deliver to them – indeed, she and a party of friends left for Stuttgart immediately after the Master's departure. I copy out for you a few words from His message because of their strange import: 'Work and strive until all regions of the world are bathed in this Light. Fear not when trouble overtakes you. You will be criticized; you will be persecuted; you will be cursed and reviled. Recall in those days what I tell you now: your triumph will be sure; your hearts will be filled with the Glory of God, for the heavenly power will sustain you, and God will be with you.'

Persecuted! What can it mean? It is perhaps as well that we meditate upon these words – useless though speculation is in the face of God's inscrutable decree – but may not our reflection upon these matters yet serve to inform our future action however implausible it may seem and remote from our present comprehension? I could not help but recall the Master's words when He spoke to us one morning in His salon. He began by apologizing for having kept His guests waiting: 'You will not mind having waited a little to see me. I have waited years and years in prison, that I might come to see you now.' And then, 'Released from my prison by the power of God, I meet here the friends of God, and I am thankful unto Him. Let us spread the Cause of God, for which I suffered persecution.' Although the Master passed along quickly to other subjects, speaking of the joy of being able to meet in freedom, those words stayed with me and I later wrote them down. I feel He was warning us that in following His path it will be the lot of some of us, in each generation, to suffer persecution for His Father's Cause.

Ada and Paul are well and are looking forward to the arrival of the baby within a matter of weeks. No doubt the birth will be a significant factor in their reconciliation with papa – an end which mamma and Maggie will foster with good faith and their not inconsiderable combined talent for preserving family unity. Maggie is an especially formidable champion of peace, and in part to this end – and no doubt in part because of her own heart's quest for truth – she is reading the Bahá'í Writings, and thus will be a knowledgeable defender of Paul and Ada if they accept the Cause. Ada has implied in her last letter that when the baby comes she and Paul would like an introduction to the Boston Bahá'í friends, and I have encouraged them to arrange this through you. I rely heavily on your affection for them, Emily, to inspire you to co-operate in this venture – nor am I forgetful of your diplomatic skills and your taste for spiritual intrigue!

A disturbing dream last night. I was in Rome, about to make my début in an opera that had been commissioned for me – a grandiose notion! But one might as well dream lavishly! I have no idea who wrote it or what it was about, but I remember being fitted for costumes with bouffant skirts and great trains and voluminous velvet cloaks and wondering how I could stagger about under their weight – then I received an urgent message from May urging me to hasten to her. I was immediately transported, as one is in dreams, to a large city – perhaps New York or Chicago; I had no sense of place – where an unimaginably sinister man was passing among the believers smiling falsely and in an unctuous manner offering them the bread of life on which he was pouring honey. I have never experienced such fear as I felt watching him, nor had I imagined there could exist in the world the atmosphere of evil that emanated from him, an unspeakable vileness, all the more horrible for his smiling face, his seeming act of charity. May beckoned and I rushed forward and linked hands with her and Juliet and several others – you and Peter were there, and Michael – and with considerable effort we made a circle, a cordon, around the man to prevent the believers reaching him. Nevertheless, a few forced their way through to him, beguiled by his mellifluous voice, but the others joined our circle or helped turn back the pressing throng. The honey, you see, was a lethal poison.

I started up from sleep shivering and sat by the window for an hour looking at the city, grey and exhausted in the moonlight. Except for a few night sounds, a dull veil of sleep covered Paris. It came to me that the Sun of Bahá'u'lláh's Revelation has dawned and yet the world sleeps on – apathetic, negligent, indifferent, chilled, and vulnerable to the evils the night conceals. *Vigilance* was the word which kept forming in my mind – the Bahá'ís must be vigilant, for the people are sleeping and dark terrors stalk the streets, as insidious as the shadows that rise up in our own minds to diminish our faith, to inflate our ambitions, to cause us to become enamored of the shimmering and seductive illusions for which we barter reality – those specters that deflect us from the purpose of our existence.

If I can find the words I should like to make a song of the idea that if we have been given an immortal soul through which we can fulfil the purpose of our human existence, to know and love the Creator of our soul, then everything that does not contribute to that purpose is – well, if not death, a detour. Michael says it would make an interesting polemic but probably a very, very bad poem. In any case, I have resolved to become more vigilant. My dream stays with me and whispers meanings in my ear.

Paris
25 January 1912

Dearest Mamma,

I have resolved to return to America and hope you will be happy about my decision. Nels and Amy Summerville have become excited about my return and are urging me to join them on the maiden voyage of the *Titanic* which leaves from England in April. If I were to sail from London I could meet aunt Edna and all could return together, as you suggest, but I am undecided as yet and in any case it might be too late now to book passage. There has been some speculation about whether 'Abbás Effendi might cross on that ship to begin His tour of America, but I think there is no foundation for those rumors. An American friend, Mr Woodcock, has invited me to join his party who are working their way towards Italy – they thought I might wish to join them in Naples where we could pick up a ship. I shall let you know the moment my plans are settled. Whatever happens, it will not be long before I am with you. I cannot wait to see you and papa – and surely I'll have a new niece or nephew to cuddle by then! Maggie will want to pronounce judgment on my physical welfare, of course, and repair any damage with her cooking. We will all have so much to talk about. I wonder whether you will find me changed beyond recognition?

Paris
24 February 1912

Dear May,

Despite the difficulty of an early birth, Ada was delivered of a lively baby girl and both are doing well. They have named her for me, and I am not unaware of the significance of this gesture.

The news of your preparations for the Master's visit is most exciting. I can well imagine your delight that Mírzá Aḥmad Sohráb's meetings in Montreal should have resulted in such excellent publicity in the leading Canadian newspaper, and these events being followed upon so quickly by Mr Honore Jaxon's tour of Montreal, Ottawa, Toronto and Quebec will surely produce results. Mr Jaxon was in London during the Master's stay there, and his work among the labor organizations and socialists was impressive. That 'Abdu'l-Bahá should be drawn to Montreal I see as a deserved result of your efforts, for your service and love are the magnet that brings this bounty.

Nels' novel is at last to be published by Michael's firm, the revisions having been agreed upon, and it is likely to be a commercial success in Michael's view. It is considered to have flashes of a shallow kind of brilliance and it challenges many time-honored, smug conventions; but its weakness may be found in its glibness and a pervasive pessimism. Michael says it was written from expert contrivance rather than experienced conviction, but it is expected to enjoy a popular reception. It has been argued by two acquaintances who read the manuscript that one of the central characters, a red-haired woman deluded by her own naive idealism, is based on Nels' view of me, and that the author took vicarious vengeance in describing her.eventual decline into bitter disillusion. I cannot believe that Nels would be deliberately unkind. Be that as it may, Nels is elated and thriving on the promised success of the book; it has enabled him to achieve stature in an élite group whose admiration he has coveted, so our paths rarely cross. He has now adopted a somewhat patronizing attitude towards the Faith, a kind of 'My dear, are you still interested in *that*?' – but despite this, our relationship in some ways seems more real and friendly than it has ever been. He no longer thinks of himself as in love with me, which opens us to a degree of relaxation never before possible; it has altered Amy's attitude, too. She is softer toward me now, almost maternal, and has almost abandoned her efforts to shock me. Nels quite likes me, but I don't interest him – in fact, I think I quite bore him – so we have little to say; but when we meet it is pleasant. We are rather like two travelers who once shared a hazardous journey; we have little in common, now that we have gone our separate ways, but hold one another in affection. It is, perhaps, in that sense, a victory for both of us. Someone recently said of Nels, 'He collects exotics, and both the

Faith and you proved to be too domestic for him, so he's taken up Freud and Amy Summerville.' Although that smacks of gossip and is one of those witticisms on which idle wags dine out for a week, it may contain a homely crumb of truth.

Nels may at a later time, perhaps in some crisis, examine the Faith again, unfettered by his need for my approval; but for the moment he has ceased to show interest in a spiritual quest and seems reinforced in his belief that the arts will provide a new direction for the human race. A somewhat exclusive and limiting philosophy, but there it is.

I wonder whether it is possible that we make our search for truth with particular intensity when we are young and resolve the 'why' questions – Why was I born? What is the purpose of existence? What is the good life? etc. – or fail to resolve them, and rarely take up the quest again. Maggie used to chide gently at my melodramatic response to adolescent crises, telling me that it was in the nature of youth to live on this level of full-blown response and to brood about life and death, and that time would teach me that the deepest griefs can be outlived. But I have seen great unhappiness in people in middle age who have evaded or unsatisfactorily resolved the basic questions – it is as though they have to meet the questions again in order to carry on with their life successfully. I sometimes wonder if my father's attacks are in some way the result of his failure to re-examine the answers he found in youth – not that those answers were wrong, but that he did not keep them alive or has outgrown them.

In earnest consultation with Prof Clémenceau I have decided against going to Rome or Stuttgart for further study. Instead I feel I should return home – certainly I want to be in America for the visit of the Master. And I must make peace with my family, do all I can to heal any wounds. I also have the feeling that the Master's journey there will be the prelude to a period of difficulty for the Cause – I don't know how to say it, but the coming of the light will cause the hawk, the owl and the bat to flee in consternation, and the foolish to raise their voices in uproar. I sense a period of confusion and difficulty, almost a sense of evil which I cannot define. I feel I should be with my family, in any case, especially since papa's health seems to be steadily deteriorating.

Oh May, what am I to do! Nels and Amy are tempting me to join them in London and cross with them to America, Nels being especially persuasive by holding out hope that through Amy's many important literary connections there I shall be given many opportunities to be – in his words, with just the smallest sneer – 'a good little missionary.' I'm not insensible of the fact that my accompanying them would lend a desirable note of respectability to their liaison which may not be based entirely on a mutual and platonic interest in belles-lettres. Or so Amy hints in those moments when she forgets her resolve to give up attempting to shock me. She is always spinning dramas and this may be just another; I doubt whether *she* believes all she says! The question of my return is vexed by my parents' insistent suggestion that my filial responsibility is to join my father's sister in England and take ship with her, joining Nels' party for the voyage. My aunt Edna, I might say, has shown no enthusiasm for the idea; she has always liked to be independent and to dart about on her own at whim. I barely know my aunt, a vague formidable figure from my early childhood, a woman with thick eyebrows and a peevish voice. I remember rustling black taffeta skirts, the smell of liniment and throat lozenges, her demand that I curtsy when greeting her. Children didn't interest her. What a bizarre party we should make! And were I to leave now, how shall Michael and I fare? To be separated from him now would be one of those minor deaths I am too cowardly to countenance. It will be some time before he can wind up his affairs and leave Paris. Would that you were here to advise me!

I hold high hopes for Michael. Recently a rainstorm interrupted an evening stroll after we had been to see Emil Cohl's film of animated drawings, and we took snug refuge in a café. Michael was in a philosophical mood and spoke of Cohl's genius which led to a discussion of the use of the intellectual faculty. I was too quick to protest some comment of Michael's and he grew silent.

'Michael,' I said, 'illumined intellect is one of our greatest powers and the strongest support of faith. Do you think I am anti-intellectual?'

'No,' he replied, 'you're a sensitive; a pre-intellectual, perhaps.'

'Stupid? Weak-minded?'

'That's not a reasonable conclusion to draw

from my comment. Yours is the way of the heart, the great shortcut. Your intellect then consolidates and elucidates your heart's findings. But that's not my way.'

Suddenly frightened, I asked, 'Michael, will you be able to reason away the Bahá'í Faith?'

He shrugged. 'All that reason destroys, hope must recreate.'

When I exclaimed that he was being ambiguous and unbearable he laughed and said, 'I have far to go before I can say that I believe in God. I'm not sure I understand what you mean when you say you do. But one begins somewhere. I believe in the good of life. I believe in you. I believe in the principles 'Abdu'l-Bahá expounds and in the uniqueness of the mission He's called to.'

I couldn't resist: 'But, Michael, you've said "I believe" three times.'

'Then I'll say it again,' he replied. '*I believe* this conversation has gone on long enough,' and we ended up laughing aloud, causing the waiter to come running to our table in alarm.

I've said little about Michael in my letters to my parents whereas I used to speak often of Nels. Strange, isn't it? But something warns me to bide.

Paris
6 March 1912

Emily, dearest –

I address just you, as you may not wish to share all of this with Peter. Imagine for the moment that we are together again in Paris and you are the patient friend who always heard me out.

It is now dawn and I am bodily weary, but my mind is in a whirl. Michael and I spent most of the night walking along the river or huddling in cafés, sometimes warming our hands over the fires of chestnut vendors, and I *think* we are engaged! I mean, we would *like* to be, but we want to obtain the Master's blessing, of course, before we really allow ourselves to believe that it has happened. And then, too, we both have many fences to mend. It seems one cannot move forward without first retracing one's steps and laying a firm foundation for further progress, healing hurts and rebuilding bridges one has rashly burned. At least that is how Michael and I feel about it, this being one of the subjects about which we unburdened our hearts in the pre-dawn hours.

It began, I think, as we strolled by the water, saying little, content to be in each other's company. The soft sluggish liquid sound of the river recalled my dream of one day making pilgrimage to the Holy Shrines and I spoke, almost to myself, of this hope. Michael asked me who might be by my side at the Thresholds – I realized he was inviting me to reveal my feelings – but before I could speak I saw that he had determined to reveal his own. In tender words he declared his love – quietly, inquisitively almost; he clearly had no idea that I had already, in my own mind, met, affirmed and reciprocated his feeling.

It was so easy at that point to feel for a few skyey minutes that had been lifted out of time a heady irresponsibility – that love makes its own laws, exonerates the lover from duty and the ties of earth, exempts the smitten heart from all the mundane obligations that regulate man, the social creature. Had Michael in that moment asked me to run off with him it would have seemed the natural course, the right and privilege of the lover. I would not have considered elopement a form of cowardice or a flouting of life's inexorable laws, a gesture of contempt flung in the grim face of the mortal death that awaits us all. Above all, I would not have admitted that it was the childish response of fear when confronted with commitment; I could even have found a spiritual justification for running away with Michael.

But as he continued to speak I realized that we might, in marriage, enter an eternal covenant, one to endure through all worlds, one to bind us in every aspect of existence without the need to reject or deny large areas of the human experience, including the most humble and tedious. In a series of rushing visions I saw myself nursing Michael through headcolds, bearing his children, growing old with him, equal partners in a mutual covenant in fulfilment of which we both might grow and develop fully our capacities – my being husbanded by him, he being espoused by me, learning what those words really mean in spiritual as well as conventional terms. This seemed so much richer and rewarding and challenging, so much more what a true marriage might be, that I could only smile and nod blindly when Michael suggested that we ask the Master's approval and supplicate that we might create a home in which would be reflected, in the family unit, the harmony to which the Bahá'í Teachings invite the nations. I'm sorry, dear, if this sounds silly and slushy and confused. Life is, isn't it? And love, too, isn't it?

Well, to go on – even as I assented (how could I not?) I sensed a reservation in Michael and he expressed it immediately; well, two, really. And yet without them I cannot imagine our love ever being able to be given its highest expression. The first was his pledge that the Faith would always be his first loyalty and he felt that I too would ask that he recognize this as my wish for both of us. I can only love him the more for knowing I felt that way.

The second reservation was his fear that I might reject him for concealing from me his Jewish background! Here, at last, his secret! I was utterly taken by surprise but it seemed irrelevant what his upbringing might have been; it was as though he had confessed that the color of his hair caused him concern or might disturb me. But it cannot be dismissed lightly, for it is a painful area of Michael's life which he feels he must turn back to in order to find his way forward.

I had not guessed Michael's story; he seemed so self-possessed, so firmly placed in the present circumstances of his life, that I had never felt great curiosity about his past. But there was always the atmosphere of secrecy about him and the shield of extreme courtesy. Michael feels that if he is to become a Bahá'í he must reclaim all that he has rejected, re-examine and re-interpret it, and incorporate into his future life all its good essence.

It hurt Michael to speak of his early life — he is deeply ashamed of his behavior toward his family and feels he must make amends. His mother died while he was an infant and he and his elder sister were raised by his father and two maiden aunts in a rather orthodox Jewish atmosphere. He remembers even as a child resenting the 'mumbo-jumbo', as he described it, of the Jewish tradition, and suffered a sense of inferiority and humiliation for being different from his school friends, few of whom were Jewish. When quite young, despite rabbinical training, he retreated into agnosticism, first arguing violently with his father, then, until Michael was able to make his way to Europe and independence, pretending to comply but secretly despising himself for doing so.

Six years ago his sister fell in love with a gentile. The family was outraged, one of the aunts being particularly vociferous, and efforts were made to dissuade the girl from marrying. At one point Michael's father even encouraged her to live with her suitor secretly for a while rather than bring disgrace upon the family. The girl refused and eloped, with Michael's encouragement. But this was too much for Michael – he accused his father of cynicism and hypocrisy and left home. One of his aunts, known for her soft heart, confided to Michael that his mother had been a gentile – the final straw! As a last gesture of breaking from the past and renouncing his father, Michael assumed his mother's maiden name, Athlone. Although he maintains an infrequent correspondence with his sister in Chicago, Michael has never again been in touch with the other members of his family. His father lives in Montreal now, where Michael spent part of his childhood, I gather. Now Michael gathers determination to exhume the past with all its pain.

How the Cause brings us full circle! Michael feels he must return to America and build a bridge of reunion to his family in order that our lives together may have their harmonious support and blessing. I would not want it any other way. So, you see, we are both outcasts, in a sense, and it will not be easy for us. I, too, have to win my family's affirmation. There are deep-rooted fears and prejudices to overcome – I cannot remember ever having met a Jew socially through my family! – but Michael and I feel that if our betrothal wins the Master's approval we shall find our way through this maze. Our love can but grow in strength in meeting this test if we adhere to spiritual principles in the process and are not pulled off course by rebellion and pride, or a desire to bend God's laws to our desires. How we in the West cherish our vaunted independence! I had always thought of it as an eminently admirable characteristic, beyond criticism, until that moment by the river when I saw that running off with Michael would be immature, the non-creative and lesser choice. Every 'virtue' seems to have both a positive and negative expression. I have looked up a note I made of some words Juliet heard from the Master's lips – I think I shall need to refer to them often in the days ahead: 'Keep My words, obey My commands, and you will marvel at the results.' His words of course are a loving description of the limits of true human freedom.

It is curious that until one meets someone who is acutely conscious of being a Jew, one is not actually self-conscious about being a gentile. Michael does not pretend that it will be easy for his family to accept me, and he is already familiar with the limitations of life in the parson's parlor. Our sincerity and mutual trust will be put to severe tests, I fear.

I am overwhelmed by a sense of urgency to return home. Mr Woodcock is pressing me to join his party aboard the *Cedric* at Naples, and holds a ticket for me. The ship departs Alexandria on March 25th and there is the most delightful speculation that our Beloved may be aboard.

I must sleep now for I am growing drowsy and my throat feels tight – perhaps I caught a chill by the river. How ignominious an ending to a so-poignant night. Ah well, God works through nature to remind us of the mortal context in which even our most elevated moments are set. Be sure that I shall cable the moment I have made fixed plans for my return. But now I shall sleep and let my soul make whatever journeys God bids it to while my tired body rests.

———

Paris
8 March 1912

Dear May,

How promptly you answered my self-pitying cry. It was that kindness, perhaps more than anything you said in your letter, that helped; for it was reflecting on your example that triggered the recollection of what you said during one of our early conversations in Paris – that the Teachings are a balance in which we must weigh all our decisions, that we must scrupulously examine our motives, plumb the Writings to find illuminating keys, and then with a prayer on our lips courageously leap into the unknown in an effort to apply the principles of our Faith rather than to diminish the soul's power for growth by attempting to reduce Bahá'u'lláh's Teachings to a mere list of prohibitions behind which we cower from spiritual expansion, preening ourselves on our pious ability to adhere rigidly to a limited course. How dare we dignify such an attitude by calling it faith? It is the five-finger exercise of the pianist that we convince ourselves is music, forgetting that the exercise is merely preparation for that rash and courageous moment in which we are released to express creatively the genuine melody of our existence.

(Oh May, why do I get carried away and find myself lecturing to you!) What I meant to say was that your letter in which you restated much that was covered in one of our early talks was more than answer to my cry – it represented the permission to grow up which I have withheld from myself through fear of responsibility and unknown consequences. You have helped, dear May, more than I can say. Each of your letters comes as a burst of light filling the dark narrow chamber of my mind. You have shed your illumination so unstintingly among us. Thinking of you, these lines came to mind; when I have smoothed them out I shall try to match them to a melody:

> An envelope is poorly fit
> To hold the power contained in it,
> And ink unworthy to inscribe
> Such thoughts as bring the soul alive.
> A coward might, surmising token,
> Leave sealed the square, mute till open,
> The heart but feeble to engage
> The love residing on a page.

In the meantime, will you think of this as 'May's Song'?

I am on the threshold of a decision and pray that it will be – if not 'the right' one, at least 'right' for me, a true one, the one our Beloved would have me make.

Threshold, I said – as though we were not on the threshold of choice at every moment. I mean that some thresholds seem higher than our stoutest shoes could dare.

I am yours, ever, May. Sleepily yours tonight, but yours.

———

Paris
9 March 1912

Dear Emily,

I formed last night before falling asleep a perilous intention, but it remains with me this morning and has grown in intensity, as if it fattened on sleep and dream. I feel a bit giddy with

183

determination – that treacherous wine! – but even as I gazed soberly into my mirror this morning, while pinning up my hair, and repeated solemnly my father's favourite warning 'risk may bring ruin', the memory of that special tone with which he always cautioned Paul and me to prudence was drowned out by a sudden music in which my own voice was raised in a spiralling 'Yes!' It seems to me that Life begins as a Yes, and then is hedged with our defiant No, or else we should be crushed beneath choices not our own, and only then are we free to say Yes once again. Am I making sense?

I am not content that my life be a partial victory. My becoming a follower of Bahá'u'lláh's was a way of saying 'no' to the tradition of my family – my 'no' to Nels' weak insistence was a less decisive victory because I shamefully vacillated out of my own frailty – it remains now to defy my parents on the matter of joining aunt Edna in London. I risk creating an irreparable breach with my family and possibly incurring the displeasure of 'Abdu'l-Bahá Who has so clearly encouraged me to be dutiful and obedient to them – I may even lose Michael. But I have resolved here to follow my heart's impulse and throw myself on God's mercy and forgiveness. I prayed last night as I have never prayed, and in a dream saw a great vessel of light bearing the Master out across the silent sea. He stood beckoning with majestic serenity on the deck, beckoning and smiling as the ship drew further away from the shore. I was pierced by a sense of unspeakable isolation and loss, and began weeping bitterly, then cast myself into the waves to swim toward that motioning hand. The water was warm and filled with singing fish which bore me, now laughing and elated, closer and closer to the luminous ship and its cargo of Gold.

The Master beckoned – I will follow.

A hundred things await attention. I must see Michael, telegraph Mr Woodcock, inform my family, and begin a round of farewells. I shall write you again as soon as details are settled.

Details! Ordinarily the very word is like a cold hand on my heart, but I shall dance through the day. Surely the mundane necessities of existence should curtsy before our heroic intentions (even if they're tiny intentions?).

Soon I shall be with you, dearest friend, soon. Before long I shall meet your Peter and we'll all be together in His presence. Soon I shall come, laden with gifts, and laughing. You'll know me by the white plume in my hat.

Yours,

Althea

Some Tributes to May Ellis Maxwell

WORDS OF 'ABDU'L-BAHÁ

'Abdu'l-Bahá during His journey and sojourn through that Dominion obtained the utmost joy. Before My departure, many souls warned Me not to travel to Montreal, saying, the majority of the inhabitants are Catholics, and are in the utmost fanaticism, that they are submerged in the sea of imitations, that they have not the capability to hearken to the call of the Kingdom of God, that the veil of bigotry has so covered the eyes that they have deprived themselves from beholding the signs of the most great guidance, and that the dogmas have taken possession of the hearts entirely, leaving no trace of reality. They asserted that should the Sun of Reality shine with perfect splendor throughout that Dominion, the dark, impenetrable clouds of superstitions have so enveloped the horizon that it would be utterly impossible for anyone to behold its rays.

But these stories did not have any effect on the resolution of 'Abdu'l-Bahá. He, trusting in God, turned His face toward Montreal. When He entered that city He observed all the doors open, He found the hearts in the utmost receptivity and the ideal power of the Kingdom of God removing every obstacle and obstruction. In the churches and meetings of that Dominion He called men to the Kingdom of God with the utmost joy, and scattered such seeds which will be irrigated with the hand of Divine Power. Undoubtedly those seeds will grow, becoming green and verdant, and many rich harvests will be gathered. In the promotion of the divine principles He found no antagonist and no adversary. The believers He met in that city were in the utmost spirituality, and attracted with the fragrances of God. He found that through the effort of the maid-servant of God, Mrs Maxwell, a number of the sons and daughters of the Kingdom in that Dominion were gathered together and associated with each other, increasing this joyous exhilaration day by day. The time of sojourn was limited to a number of days, but the results in the future are inexhaustible. When a farmer comes into the possession of a virgin soil, in a short time he will bring under cultivation a large field. Therefore I hope that in the future Montreal may become so stirred, that the melody of the Kingdom may travel to all parts of the world from that Dominion and the breaths of the Holy Spirit may spread from that center to the East and the West of America.

Tablets of the Divine Plan
(Tablet to the Bahá'ís of
Canada, 21 February 1917)

No sooner had one of these pilgrims [the first to reach the Holy Land from the West, in 1898], the aforementioned May Bolles, returned to Paris than she succeeded, in compliance with 'Abdu'l-Bahá's emphatic instructions, in establishing in that city the first Bahá'í center to be formed on the European continent . . . in 1902, May Bolles, now married to a Canadian [William Sutherland Maxwell], transferred her residence to Montreal, and succeeded in laying the foundations of the Cause in that Dominion.

God Passes By, pp. 259, 260.

To May Maxwell, laid to rest in the soil of Argentina; to Hyde Dunn, whose dust reposes in the Antipodes, in the city of Sydney; to Keith Ransom-Kehler, entombed in distant Iṣfahán; to Susan Moody and Lillian Kappes and their valiant associates who lie buried in Ṭihrán; to Lua Getsinger, reposing forever in the capital of Egypt, and last but not least to Martha Root, interred in an island in the bosom of the Pacific, belong the matchless honor of having conferred, through their services and sacrifice, a lustre upon the American Bahá'í community for which its representatives, while celebrating at their historic, their first All-American Convention, their hard-won victories, may well feel eternally grateful.

ibid., p. 400.

In Memoriam

'Abdu'l-Bahá's beloved handmaid, the distinguished disciple, May Maxwell, is gathered into
the glory of the Abhá Kingdom. Her earthly life,
so rich, eventful, incomparably blessed, is worthily
ended. To sacred tie her signal services had forged,
the priceless honor of a martyr's death is now
added, a double crown deservedly won. The
Seven Year Plan [and] particularly the South
American campaign derives fresh impetus from
the example of her glorious sacrifice. Southern
outpost of Faith greatly enriched through association with her historic resting place, destined to
remain a poignant reminder of the resistless
march of the triumphant army of Bahá'u'lláh.
Advise believers of both Americas to hold befitting memorial gathering.

3 March 1940
Messages to America, p. 38

And now as this year, so memorable in the annals
of the Faith, was drawing to a close, there befell
the American Bahá'í community, through the
dramatic and sudden death of May Maxwell, yet
another loss, which viewed in retrospect will
come to be regarded as a potent blessing conferred
upon the campaign now being so diligently
conducted by its members. Laden with the fruits
garnered through well-nigh half a century of
toilsome service to the Cause she so greatly loved,
heedless of the warnings of age and ill-health, and
afire with the longing to worthily demonstrate
her gratitude in her overwhelming awareness of

the bounties of her Lord and Master, she set her face towards the southern outpost of the Faith in the New World and laid down her life in such a spirit of consecration and self-sacrifice as has truly merited the crown of martyrdom.

To Keith Ransom-Kehler, whose dust sleeps in far-off Iṣfahán; to Martha Root, fallen in her tracks on an island in the midmost heart of the ocean; to May Maxwell, lying in solitary glory in the southern outpost of the Western Hemisphere – to these three heroines of the Formative Age of the Faith of Bahá'u'lláh, they who now labor so assiduously for its expansion and establishment, owe a debt of gratitude which future generations will not fail to adequately recognize.

ibid., 15 April 1940